Preface	4
1. Introduction to Vue.js	7
1.1 What is Vue.js?	8
1.2 The Evolution of Front-End Frameworks	13
1.3 Key Features of Vue.js	18
1.4 Setting Up the Development Environment	27
2. Getting Started with Vue CLI	31
2.1 Installing Vue CLI	32
2.2 Creating a New Project	35
2.3 Understanding the Project Structure	39
2.4 Running and Debugging Your Project	44
3. Understanding Vue Components	49
3.1 Introduction to Vue Components	50
3.2 Component Registration and Usage	54
3.3 Single File Components	58
3.4 Communication Between Components	63
4. State Management with Vuex	70
4.1 Introduction to Vuex	71
4.2 State, Getters, and Mutations	75
4.3 Actions and Modules	79
4.4 Best Practices for State Management	83
5. Vue Router for Single Page Applications	91
5.1 Basics of Vue Router	92
5.2 Dynamic Routing	97
5.3 Navigation Guards	100
5.4 Lazy Loading Routes	104

6. Vue Directives, Filters, and Mixins — 108

- 6.1 Introduction to Vue Directives — 109
- 6. Vue Directives, Filters, and Mixins — 112
- 6.3 Custom Directives in Vue.js — 116
- 6.4 Filters and Mixins: Enhancing Reusability — 122

7. Handling Forms and User Input in Vue — 127

- 7.1. Introduction to Forms in Vue — 128
- 7.2. Binding User Input with v-model — 132
- 7.3. Form Validation Methods — 140
- 7.4. Handling Form Submissions — 149

8. Integrating Vue with Laravel and Other Backend Frameworks — 156

- 8.1 Setting Up a Laravel Backend for Vue Integration — 157
- 8.2 Using Laravel APIs with Vue Components — 161
- 8.3 Integrating Vue with Other Backend Frameworks — 168
- 8.4 Common Issues and Solutions in Integrating Vue with Backends — 174

9. Testing and Debugging Vue Applications — 179

- 9.1 Understanding the Basics of Testing in Vue.js — 180
- 9.2 Writing Unit Tests for Vue Components — 184
- 9.3 Performing End-to-End Testing with Vue.js — 191
- 9.4 Debugging Common Issues in Vue Applications — 195

10. Performance Optimization Techniques — 200

- 10.1 Code Splitting — 201
- 10.2 Lazy Loading — 206
- 10.3 Memoization — 210
- 10.4 Optimizing Dependencies — 215

11. Deploying Vue Applications — 220

- 11.1. Preparing the Production Build — 221

11.2. Server Configurations for Vue Apps	225
11.3. Deploying to Cloud Providers	230
11.4. Continuous Deployment with CI/CD	234

12. Glossary — 238

Glossary — 239

Preface

Welcome to **Practical Vue.js for Modern Web Development**!

As we stand on the precipice of an ever-evolving digital landscape, the demand for highly interactive and dynamic web applications has never been higher. Vue.js, an open-source JavaScript framework, has emerged as a favored tool among developers for crafting compelling user interfaces and single-page applications with ease and efficiency.

This book was generated by artificial intelligence to serve as a comprehensive guide for anyone looking to harness the power of Vue.js. Whether you are a novice eager to dive into the world of front-end development or a seasoned developer seeking to refine your techniques, this book promises to be a valuable resource.

Why This Book?

The decision to compile this book stems from the recognition of Vue.js's growing popularity and the need for a systematic and practical resource that can address the diverse requirements of modern web development. This book aims to bridge the gap between theoretical knowledge and real-world application, providing readers with actionable insights and hands-on experience.

Through twelve meticulously structured chapters, we will explore the multifaceted world of Vue.js:

1. **Introduction to Vue.js** - Discover the fundamentals of Vue.js and understand why it stands out among other JavaScript frameworks.
2. **Getting Started with Vue CLI** - Learn how to set up your development environment using the Vue CLI for efficient project scaffolding.

3. **Understanding Vue Components** - Dive into the building blocks of Vue applications and learn to create reusable components.
4. **State Management with Vuex** - Master the art of managing complex state in large Vue applications using Vuex.
5. **Vue Router for Single Page Applications** - Explore how to implement client-side routing to develop seamless single-page applications.
6. **Vue Directives, Filters, and Mixins** - Enhance your Vue applications with custom directives, filters, and mixins for added functionality.
7. **Handling Forms and User Input in Vue** - Gain proficiency in handling user input and managing forms in your Vue applications.
8. **Integrating Vue with Laravel and Other Backend Frameworks** - Understand how to integrate Vue with backend frameworks like Laravel for full-stack development.
9. **Testing and Debugging Vue Applications** - Discover strategies and tools for testing and debugging to ensure the reliability and performance of your applications.
10. **Performance Optimization Techniques** - Learn techniques to optimize the performance of your Vue applications for a better user experience.
11. **Deploying Vue Applications** - Get to grips with best practices for deploying Vue applications to production.
12. **Glossary** - A handy glossary to help you understand the key terms and concepts used throughout the book.

Our hope is that by the end of this journey, you will not only be equipped with in-depth knowledge of Vue.js but also the confidence to leverage it in creating sophisticated and efficient web applications.

Let's get started on an exciting journey to mastering Vue.js for modern web development!

Thank you for embarking on this journey with us. We are thrilled to be a part of your learning experience and look forward to seeing the incredible applications you will build using Vue.js.

1. Introduction to Vue.js

1.1 What is Vue.js?

Vue.js is a progressive JavaScript framework used for building user interfaces and single-page applications (SPAs). Created by Evan You and first released in 2014, Vue.js has quickly gained popularity due to its simplicity, flexibility, and the power it offers to developers for building interactive web applications.

The Philosophy of Vue.js

Vue.js is designed to be incrementally adoptable. This means you can start using it to enhance parts of an HTML page with interactive components and then scale up to building complex, fully-featured SPAs. The core library focuses on the view layer only, making it easy to integrate with other libraries or existing projects. Moreover, Vue is known for its gentle learning curve, which makes it accessible for beginners while still being robust enough for advanced tasks.

The Basics of Vue.js

Vue.js allows you to declaratively bind data to the DOM using a simple and readable syntax. This can be accomplished with a template syntax that is reminiscent of HTML.

Here is a basic example of a Vue.js application:

```html
<!DOCTYPE html>
<html>
<head>
  <title>Vue.js Example</title>
  <script src="https://cdn.jsdelivr.net/npm/vue@2"></script>
</head>
<body>
  <div id="app">
    {{ message }}
  </div>

  <script>
    new Vue({
      el: '#app',
      data: {
        message: 'Hello, Vue.js!'
      }
    });
  </script>
</body>
</html>
```

In this simple example:

- We include the Vue.js library via a CDN.
- We define a Vue instance that is bound to a DOM element with the id of #app.
- The data property in the Vue instance contains a message which is interpolated into the template using the {{ message }} syntax.

Declarative Rendering

Vue.js provides a declarative syntax for dynamically updating the DOM based on the state of your application. With Vue, you describe **what** should happen, and Vue takes care of updating the DOM to match your data.

Consider the following example to demonstrate how Vue handles data binding and event handling:

```html
<!DOCTYPE html>
<html>
<head>
  <title>Vue.js Counter</title>
  <script src="https://cdn.jsdelivr.net/npm/vue@2"></script>
</head>
<body>
  <div id="counter-app">
    <button @click="counter++">You clicked me {{ counter }} times.</button>
  </div>

  <script>
    new Vue({
      el: '#counter-app',
      data: {
        counter: 0
      }
    });
  </script>
</body>
</html>
```

In this example:

- The `@click` directive binds a click event to the button.
- When the button is clicked, the `counter` data property is incremented.
- The button's text dynamically updates to reflect the state of the `counter` property.

Components

At the heart of Vue.js are components. Components are Vue instances with predefined options. They allow you to create reusable blocks of code, which can be nested and composed to build complex UIs.

Here is an example of a simple Vue component:

```
<!DOCTYPE html>
<html>
<head>
  <title>Vue.js Components</title>
  <script src="https://cdn.jsdelivr.net/npm/vue@2"></script>
</head>
<body>
  <div id="app">
    <greeting></greeting>
  </div>

  <script>
    Vue.component('greeting', {
      template: '<h1>Hello, Vue Component!</h1>'
    });

    new Vue({
      el: '#app'
    });
  </script>
</body>
</html>
```

In this example:

- We define a new component called `greeting` using `Vue.component`.
- The `template` option specifies the HTML that will be rendered.
- We then use the `greeting` component within our main Vue instance.

Why Choose Vue.js?

Vue.js strikes a balance between ease of use and powerful features. Some compelling reasons to choose Vue.js include:

- **Ease of Learning**: The core concepts are simple to grasp for beginners.

- **Flexibility**: You can use it as a library to enhance specific parts of your application or as a full-fledged framework for building complex SPAs.
- **Rich Ecosystem**: Vue.js comes with a host of official libraries and tools, such as Vue Router for routing and Vuex for state management, enabling you to build large-scale applications.

Vue.js is designed to help you build modern web applications with ease. Understanding its core principles and using its powerful features will set a strong foundation for your journey into modern web development.

1.2 The Evolution of Front-End Frameworks

To fully appreciate the capabilities and strengths of Vue.js, it's vital to understand the landscape of front-end development from which it emerged. The evolution of front-end frameworks has been driven by the necessity to create highly interactive and seamless user experiences. Let's take a journey through the development of front-end frameworks and see how they have shaped modern web development.

The Early Days of JavaScript

In the initial days of web development, JavaScript was primarily used to make web pages more interactive and user-friendly. Dynamic features such as form validations, image sliders, and basic user interactions were script-based and embedded directly into HTML files. However, as web applications grew more complex, this approach quickly became unmanageable.

```
<!DOCTYPE html>
<html>
<head>
    <title>Simple JavaScript Example</title>
</head>
<body>
    <button onclick="alertMessage()">Click Me</button>

    <script>
        function alertMessage() {
            alert("Hello, this is a JavaScript alert!");
        }
    </script>
</body>
</html>
```

The Rise of jQuery

jQuery, introduced in 2006, revolutionized front-end development by simplifying the process of DOM manipulation, event handling, and AJAX calls. Its concise syntax allowed developers to write less code to achieve more functionalities. This led to jQuery becoming one of the most popular JavaScript libraries in the late 2000s.

```html
<!DOCTYPE html>
<html>
<head>
    <title>jQuery Example</title>
    <script src="https://code.jquery.com/jquery-3.6.0.min.js"></script>
</head>
<body>
    <button id="myButton">Click Me</button>

    <script>
        $(document).ready(function(){
            $("#myButton").click(function(){
                alert("Hello, this is a jQuery alert!");
            });
        });
    </script>
</body>
</html>
```

The Emergence of MVC Frameworks

As web applications continued to grow in complexity, the need for more structured and scalable solutions became evident. This led to the emergence of Model-View-Controller (MVC) frameworks such as AngularJS, introduced by Google in 2010. AngularJS allowed for two-way data binding, dependency injection, and a component-based architecture, making it easier to build maintainable and testable applications.

```html
<!DOCTYPE html>
<html ng-app="myApp">
<head>
    <title>AngularJS Example</title>
    <script src="https://ajax.googleapis.com/ajax/libs/angularjs/1.8.2/angular.min.js"></script>
</head>
<body>
    <div ng-controller="MyController">
        <input type="text" ng-model="message">
        <p>{{ message }}</p>
    </div>

    <script>
        var app = angular.module('myApp', []);
        app.controller('MyController', function($scope) {
            $scope.message = "Hello, AngularJS!";
        });
    </script>
</body>
</html>
```

The Component-Based Revolution

React, developed by Facebook and introduced in 2013, brought a paradigm shift by embracing a component-based architecture and a virtual DOM. React's ability to encapsulate state and behavior within reusable components allowed developers to build highly interactive and efficient user interfaces. The concept of unidirectional data flow also improved the predictability of application state management.

```html
<!DOCTYPE html>
<html>
<head>
    <title>React Example</title>
</head>
<body>
    <div id="root"></div>

    <script src="https://unpkg.com/react/umd/react.development.js"></script>
    <script src="https://unpkg.com/react-dom/umd/react-dom.development.js"></script>

    <script>
        class App extends React.Component {
            constructor(props) {
                super(props);
                this.state = { message: "Hello, React!" };
            }

            render() {
                return <div>{this.state.message}</div>;
            }
        }

        ReactDOM.render(<App />, document.getElementById('root'));
    </script>
</body>
</html>
```

The Advent of Vue.js

Vue.js, created by Evan You and released in 2014, combined the best features of Angular and React, such as the reactive data binding of Angular and the component architecture of React. Vue's gentle learning curve, ease of integration, and flexibility in leveraging both React's and Angular's best practices made it an attractive choice for developers of all skill levels. Vue's ecosystem quickly evolved to include powerful tools like Vue Router for routing and Vuex for state management, further extending its capabilities.

```
<!DOCTYPE html>
<html>
<head>
    <title>Vue.js Example</title>
    <script src="https://cdn.jsdelivr.net/npm/vue@2.6.14/dist/vue.js"></script>
</head>
<body>
    <div id="app">
        <input v-model="message" />
        <p>{{ message }}</p>
    </div>

    <script>
        new Vue({
            el: '#app',
            data: {
                message: 'Hello, Vue.js!'
            }
        });
    </script>
</body>
</html>
```

Conclusion

From the rudimentary days of scripting to the sophisticated frameworks we use today, front-end development has undergone significant transformations. Each evolutionary step addressed the growing demands for more interactive, maintainable, and scalable web applications. Vue.js, with its versatility and efficiency, represents the culmination of these advancements, providing a robust framework for modern web development. In the next section, we will delve deeper into the unique features that set Vue.js apart from other frameworks.

1.3 Key Features of Vue.js

Vue.js is a progressive JavaScript framework used for building user interfaces and single-page applications. It offers a variety of features that make it a potent tool for modern web development. Below, we explore some of the key features of Vue.js, accompanied by practical code examples.

Reactive Data Binding

One of the standout features of Vue.js is its reactivity system, which ensures that the UI stays in sync with the underlying data model. This is achieved through reactive data binding.

```
<div id="app">
  <p>{{ message }}</p>
</div>

<script>
  const app = new Vue({
    el: '#app',
    data: {
      message: 'Hello Vue!'
    }
  });
</script>
```

In this example, any change to `app.message` will automatically update the HTML content.

Vue Components

Vue.js allows you to encapsulate reusable pieces of UI into components. Components are fundamental to building large-scale applications.

```
<template id="my-component">
  <div>
    <h1>{{ title }}</h1>
    <p>This is a reusable component</p>
  </div>
</template>

<script>
  Vue.component('my-component', {
    template: '#my-component',
    data() {
      return {
        title: 'My Component'
      };
    }
  });

  new Vue({ el: '#app' });
</script>

<div id="app">
  <my-component></my-component>
</div>
```

Directives

Vue.js comes with a set of built-in directives like `v-if`, `v-for`, and `v-bind` that enhance the functionality of your templates.

```
<div id="app">
  <p v-if="isVisible">Now you see me</p>
  <p v-else>Now you don't</p>
  <ul>
    <li v-for="item in items" :key="item.id">{{ item.name }
}</li>
  </ul>
</div>

<script>
  new Vue({
    el: '#app',
    data: {
      isVisible: true,
      items: [
        { id: 1, name: 'Item One' },
        { id: 2, name: 'Item Two' }
      ]
    }
  });
</script>
```

Computed Properties

Computed properties are like reactive data that can be derived from other reactive data. They are cached based on dependencies and only re-evaluate when necessary.

```
<div id="app">
  <p>Original message: {{ message }}</p>
  <p>Reversed message: {{ reversedMessage }}</p>
</div>

<script>
  new Vue({
    el: '#app',
    data: {
      message: 'Hello Vue!'
    },
    computed: {
      reversedMessage() {
        return this.message.split('').reverse().join('');
      }
    }
  });
</script>
```

Watchers

Vue.js provides a watch option to perform asynchronous operations or compute expensive properties, in an efficient way when the data changes.

```
<div id="app">
  <input v-model="question" placeholder="Ask a question">
  <p>{{ answer }}</p>
</div>

<script>
  new Vue({
    el: '#app',
    data: {
      question: '',
      answer: 'I cannot give you an answer until you ask a question!'
    },
    watch: {
      question(newQuestion) {
        this.answer = 'Waiting for you to stop typing...';
        this.getAnswer(newQuestion);
      }
    },
    methods: {
      getAnswer(question) {
        if (question.indexOf('?') === -1) {
          this.answer = 'Questions usually contain a question mark ;-)';
          return;
        }
        this.answer = 'Thinking...';
        setTimeout(() => {
          this.answer = 'I got it!';
        }, 500);
      }
    }
  });
</script>
```

Vue Router

Vue Router is the official router for Vue.js, making it easy to create single-page applications with navigation and routing.

```
<div id="app">
  <router-view></router-view>
</div>

<script>
  const Home = { template: '<div>Home</div>' };
  const About = { template: '<div>About</div>' };

  const routes = [
    { path: '/home', component: Home },
    { path: '/about', component: About }
  ];

  const router = new VueRouter({
    routes
  });

  new Vue({
    el: '#app',
    router
  });
</script>
```

Vuex

Vuex is the state management library for Vue.js, allowing you to manage complex state in a more structured way.

```js
const store = new Vuex.Store({
  state: {
    count: 0
  },
  mutations: {
    increment(state) {
      state.count++;
    }
  }
});

new Vue({
  el: '#app',
  store,
  computed: {
    count() {
      return this.$store.state.count;
    }
  },
  methods: {
    increment() {
      this.$store.commit('increment');
    }
  }
});
```

Transition Effects

Vue.js provides a system for applying CSS transitions when elements enter or leave the DOM.

```html
<div id="app">
  <button @click="show = !show">Toggle</button>
  <transition name="fade">
    <p v-if="show">Hello Vue.js!</p>
  </transition>
</div>

<script>
  new Vue({
    el: '#app',
    data: {
      show: true
    }
  });
</script>

<style>
  .fade-enter-active, .fade-leave-active {
    transition: opacity 0.5s;
  }
  .fade-enter, .fade-leave-to {
    opacity: 0;
  }
</style>
```

Integration with Other Libraries

Vue.js can be easily integrated with other libraries or existing projects, providing flexibility in technology stacks.

```html
<script src="https://cdn.jsdelivr.net/npm/vue"></script>
<script src="https://cdn.jsdelivr.net/npm/axios/dist/axios.
min.js"></script>

<div id="app">
  <button @click="fetchData">Fetch Data</button>
  <p>{{ info }}</p>
</div>

<script>
  new Vue({
    el: '#app',
    data: {
      info: ''
    },
    methods: {
      fetchData() {
        axios.get('https://api.example.com/data')
        .then(response => {
          this.info = response.data;
        });
      }
    }
  });
</script>
```

With these robust features, Vue.js stands out in the crowded space of JavaScript frameworks, providing a developer-friendly approach to building dynamic and efficient web applications.

1.4 Setting Up the Development Environment

To start developing with Vue.js, it's crucial to set up your development environment correctly. Proper setup ensures that you can harness the full potential of Vue.js and streamline your development process. This subchapter will guide you through the essential tools and steps required for setting up a Vue.js development environment.

Prerequisites

Before diving into the setup, ensure that you have the following prerequisites installed on your machine:

13. **Node.js**: Vue.js requires Node.js to run the Vue CLI and manage project dependencies.
14. **npm or Yarn**: These are package managers that come with Node.js (npm) or can be installed separately (Yarn).

Checking Node.js and npm Versions

You can verify the installation and check the versions of Node.js and npm using the following commands:

```
node -v
npm -v
```

Installing Node.js

If Node.js is not installed on your system, you can download it from the official website and follow the installation instructions:

- Download Node.js: https://nodejs.org/

Updating npm

If you already have Node.js installed, it's essential to ensure that npm is up to date. You can update npm to the latest version using the following command:

```
npm install -g npm
```

Installing Vue CLI

Vue CLI is a powerful tool that provides a standard setup for Vue.js applications. It streamlines project creation and configuration, making it easier to get started with Vue.js.

To install Vue CLI globally, run the following command:

```
npm install -g @vue/cli
```

You can verify the installation and check the version of Vue CLI with:

```
vue --version
```

Creating a New Vue Project

With Vue CLI installed, you can create a new Vue project effortlessly. Navigate to the directory where you want to create your project and run:

```
vue create my-vue-app
```

The CLI will prompt you to pick a preset. For beginners, it's recommended to choose the default preset with Babel and ESLint. You can navigate through the prompts and customize your project configuration.

Project Structure

After the project is created, you'll have a directory with the following structure:

```
my-vue-app/
├── node_modules/
├── public/
├── src/
│   ├── assets/
│   ├── components/
│   ├── App.vue
│   └── main.js
├── .gitignore
├── babel.config.js
├── package.json
├── README.md
└── yarn.lock (or package-lock.json)
```

Here's a brief overview of the main directories and files:

- **src/**: Contains the source code of your Vue application.
- **public/**: Includes static assets.
- **App.vue**: The root Vue component.
- **main.js**: The entry point of your application, where your Vue instance is created.

Running the Development Server

To start the development server and see your application in action, navigate to your project directory and run:

```
npm run serve
```

This will start the local development server, and you can open your browser and navigate to `http://localhost:8080` to view your application.

Code Example: Basic Vue Component

Here's a simple example of a Vue component to help you get started:

```
<template>
  <div>
    <h1>{{ message }}</h1>
  </div>
</template>

<script>
export default {
  data() {
    return {
      message: "Hello, Vue.js!"
    };
  }
};
</script>

<style scoped>
h1 {
  color: #42b983;
}
</style>
```

Conclusion

By following these steps, you've set up a complete development environment for Vue.js. With Node.js, Vue CLI, and a basic understanding of the project structure, you are now ready to start building powerful and dynamic web applications using Vue.js. In the next chapter, we will dive deeper into getting started with Vue CLI to further enhance your development workflow.

2. Getting Started with Vue CLI

2.1 Installing Vue CLI

In this section, we will cover how to install Vue CLI to get you started on your journey with Vue.js. Vue CLI (Command Line Interface) is a powerful tool that facilitates the rapid development of Vue applications by providing a project scaffolding and a host of built-in functionalities.

Prerequisites

Before installing Vue CLI, you need to have Node.js and npm (Node Package Manager) installed on your machine. You can download Node.js, which includes npm, from the official website: https://nodejs.org/.

To check if Node.js and npm are installed on your system, run the following commands in your terminal or command prompt:

```
node -v
npm -v
```

Installing Vue CLI

Vue CLI is distributed as an npm package. To install it globally on your system, run:

```
npm install -g @vue/cli
```

The -g flag stands for "global," which means Vue CLI will be available system-wide.

Verifying Vue CLI Installation

After the installation is complete, you can verify that Vue CLI is installed by checking its version. Run the following command:

```
vue --version
```

If the installation was successful, you will see the version number of Vue CLI displayed in your terminal.

Update Vue CLI

If you already have Vue CLI installed and wish to update to the latest version, run:

```
npm update -g @vue/cli
```

This command will update Vue CLI to its latest stable release.

Common Issues

Permission Denied on MacOS/Linux

If you encounter a "permission denied" error during installation, you can solve this issue by using sudo:

```
sudo npm install -g @vue/cli
```

However, using sudo should be your last resort. It's better to fix the underlying permission issues with npm. Refer to the following guide for more details: https://docs.npmjs.com/resolving-eacces-permissions-errors-when-installing-packages-globally.

Proxy Issues

If you're behind a corporate firewall or proxy, you might need to configure npm to use your proxy settings. You can set the proxy by running:

```
npm config set proxy http://your-proxy-url:port
npm config set https-proxy http://your-proxy-url:port
```

Replace `http://your-proxy-url:port` with your actual proxy settings.

Conclusion

You now have Vue CLI installed and are ready to start building Vue applications. In the next section, we will guide you through creating a new Vue project using Vue CLI and explore its project structure. Proceed to section 2.2 to continue your learning journey.

2.2 Creating a New Project

In this subchapter, we'll walk through the steps necessary to create a new Vue.js project using the Vue CLI. The Vue CLI significantly streamlines the setup process, ensuring that your project is ready for modern web development out of the box. Let's dive in!

Initializing a New Project

Once Vue CLI is installed, initializing a new project is straightforward. Open your terminal and navigate to the directory where you want to create your new project. From there, run the following command:

```
vue create my-new-project
```

Replace `my-new-project` with the desired name for your project. This command will trigger an interactive prompt to guide you through the project setup.

Choosing Presets and Manual Configurations

The Vue CLI offers a couple of options: - **Default Preset**: Quickly set up a project with default configuration, including Babel, ESLint, and more. - **Manually select features**: Provides an opportunity to customize the configuration to suit your specific needs.

For most custom setups, you'll want to manually select features. Here's an example of the interactive prompts you might encounter:

```
? Please pick a preset:
  Default ([Vue 2] babel, eslint)
  Default (Vue 3) ([Vue 3] babel, eslint)
❯ Manually select features
```

When you choose to manually select features, you'll be asked to pick the technologies and tools you want included, such as TypeScript, Progressive Web App (PWA) support, Vue Router, Vuex, CSS preprocessors, and Linter/Formatter.

Example Configuration

After choosing to manually select features, you might see a series of prompts like the following:

```
? Check the features needed for your project: (Press <space
> to select, <a> to toggle all, <i> to invert selection)
 ○ Choose Vue version
 ○ Babel
 ○ TypeScript
 ○ Progressive Web App (PWA) Support
 ○ Router
 ○ Vuex
 ○ CSS Pre-processors
 ○ Linter / Formatter
 ○ Unit Testing
 ○ E2E Testing
```

Using the arrow keys, space bar, and enter key, select the features that match your requirements. Let's say we selected Router, Vuex, and CSS Pre-processors. Next, you might encounter specific configuration choices for each tool.

Configuring Vue Router and Vuex

For example, if you chose Vue Router and Vuex, you might see:

```
? Use history mode for router? (Requires proper server setu
p for index fallback in production): (Y/n) Y
```

```
? Pick a CSS pre-processor (PostCSS, Autoprefixer and CSS M
odules are supported by default):
  Sass/SCSS
  Dart Sass
  Node Sass
  Less
  Stylus
```

Select the appropriate options based on your project's needs. After answering the prompts, the Vue CLI will create your project with the configured settings.

Finalizing the Setup

Once all configurations are set, the CLI will create the project and install the necessary dependencies. This can take a few minutes. Upon completion, navigate into your project directory and run the following command to open your project in a code editor. For example, if you're using Visual Studio Code:

```
cd my-new-project
code .
```

Starting the Development Server

With your project set up, you can run the development server to see your application in action:

```
npm run serve
```

This command starts a local development server, and you can view your project by opening a browser and visiting http://localhost:8080.

Summary

Creating a new Vue.js project with the Vue CLI simplifies the setup process, allowing you to focus directly on development. By following the steps above, you can efficiently configure your project with all the necessary tools and start building your modern web application in Vue.js.

In the next subchapter, we'll delve into understanding the project structure, so you can get familiar with the various files and directories generated by the Vue CLI.

2.3 Understanding the Project Structure

After creating a new Vue.js project using Vue CLI, it's essential to understand the structure of the generated files and directories. This foundation will help you navigate the project efficiently and make logical modifications as needed.

Project Root Directory

At the root level of your project, you will find several files and directories. Here's a brief overview of the most commonly found items:

- `node_modules/`: This directory contains all the Node.js modules required by the project. It is generated and managed by npm/yarn.
- `public/`: This directory holds the public assets for the project, such as `index.html` and static files.
- `src/`: This is where your application code resides. It includes the main application file and folders for components, views, and more.
- `.gitignore`: Specifies which files and directories to ignore in version control.
- `babel.config.js`: Configuration file for Babel, a JavaScript compiler.
- `package.json`: Lists project dependencies and scripts.

Key Files and Directories

Let's explore some specific directories and files that are crucial to a Vue.js project created by Vue CLI.

package.json

This is a JSON file that holds metadata about the project, including the list of dependencies, scripts to run tasks, and other configurations. Here's a typical view of the package.json file:

```
{
  "name": "my-vue-project",
  "version": "1.0.0",
  "private": true,
  "scripts": {
    "serve": "vue-cli-service serve",
    "build": "vue-cli-service build",
    "lint": "vue-cli-service lint"
  },
  "dependencies": {
    "vue": "^3.0.0"
  },
  "devDependencies": {
    "@vue/cli-service": "~4.5.12",
    "@vue/cli-plugin-babel": "~4.5.12",
    "eslint": "^6.7.2"
  }
}
```

babel.config.js

This file configures Babel in your Vue.js project. Babel is used to transpile modern JavaScript so it can run in older browsers. Here's an example content of babel.config.js:

```
module.exports = {
  presets: [
    '@vue/cli-plugin-babel/preset'
  ]
}
```

src Directory

The src/ directory contains your main application code. Let's break down some critical files and folders:

- `main.js`: The entry file for the application. This is where Vue is initialized.
- `App.vue`: The root component of your application.
- `components/`: This folder is where your Vue components reside.
- `assets/`: Contains the static assets like images and fonts.
- `views/`: Houses the view components for different routes in your application (if you are using Vue Router).

main.js

This file initializes your Vue instance and mounts it to the `#app` element in `public/index.html`.

```
import { createApp } from 'vue'
import App from './App.vue'

createApp(App).mount('#app')
```

App.vue

This is the root component of your application. It's a single-file component with three parts: `<template>`, `<script>`, and `<style>`.

```vue
<template>
  <div id="app">
    <img alt="Vue logo" src="./assets/logo.png">
    <HelloWorld msg="Welcome to Your Vue.js App"/>
  </div>
</template>

<script>
import HelloWorld from './components/HelloWorld.vue'

export default {
  name: 'App',
  components: {
    HelloWorld
  }
}
</script>

<style>
#app {
  font-family: Avenir, Helvetica, Arial, sans-serif;
  text-align: center;
  color: #2c3e50;
  margin-top: 60px;
}
</style>
```

components/HelloWorld.vue

An example component provided by the Vue CLI when you create a new project. It usually serves as the initial structure of your project and can be modified or deleted as you develop your application.

```vue
<template>
  <div class="hello">
    <h1>{{ msg }}</h1>
  </div>
</template>

<script>
export default {
  name: 'HelloWorld',
  props: {
    msg: String
  }
}
</script>

<style scoped>
h1 {
  font-weight: normal;
}
</style>
```

Conclusion

Understanding the Vue CLI project structure is essential for efficient and effective development. This guided tour of the main files and directories provides a clear roadmap for navigating the generated project, making it easier to build a scalable and maintainable application. Taking the time to familiarize yourself with this structure will pay dividends as you progress in your Vue.js development journey.

2.4 Running and Debugging Your Project

Now that you've installed Vue CLI, created a new project, and familiarized yourself with the project structure, it's time to run and debug it. This step is essential for iterative development as you'll frequently test your work to ensure everything functions correctly.

Running Your Vue Project

The Vue CLI provides a simple command to serve your project during development. This command sets up a local development server with hot-reloading, meaning your changes automatically reflect in the browser without needing a manual refresh.

To run your Vue project, open your terminal, navigate to your project root directory, and execute the following command:

```
npm run serve
```

If you're using Yarn, use:

```
yarn serve
```

This command will output something like the following:

```
DONE  Compiled successfully in 2187ms
2:58:02 PM

  App running at:
  - Local:   http://localhost:8080/
  - Network: http://192.168.0.103:8080/
```

Navigate to `http://localhost:8080/` in your web browser to see your running application.

Debugging Your Vue Project

Debugging is a critical part of the development process. Vue CLI projects come with built-in support for modern debugging tools.

Using Browser Developer Tools

Most modern web browsers come with built-in developer tools that you can use to inspect and debug your Vue application.

15. **Open Developer Tools:**
    - In Google Chrome: Right-click on the page, choose "Inspect" or press `Ctrl+Shift+I`.
    - In Firefox: Right-click on the page, choose "Inspect Element" or press `Ctrl+Shift+I`.

16. **Inspect Elements & Components:**
    - Use the "Elements" or "Inspector" tab to inspect the DOM.
    - Navigate to the "Console" tab to see any error messages or `console.log` outputs.

Using Vue Devtools

Vue Devtools is a browser extension that provides enhanced inspection capabilities for Vue.js applications.

17. **Installing Vue Devtools:**
    - For Chrome: Go to https://chrome.google.com/webstore, search for "Vue.js devtools", and install.
    - For Firefox: Go to https://addons.mozilla.org, search for "Vue.js devtools", and install.

18. **Using Vue Devtools:**
    - Once installed, open the developer tools in your browser.

- You will see a new tab labeled "Vue". Click it to inspect Vue components, Vuex state, and more.

Adding Debug Statements

You may often want to add debug statements to your code to log out values and check their state during execution. This can be easily done using `console.log()`.

```
// ExampleComponent.vue
<template>
  <div>
    <button @click="incrementCounter">Increment Counter</button>
    <p>Counter: {{ counter }}</p>
  </div>
</template>

<script>
export default {
  data() {
    return {
      counter: 0,
    };
  },
  methods: {
    incrementCounter() {
      this.counter++;
      console.log('Counter incremented to:', this.counter); // Debug statement
    },
  },
};
</script>
```

Setting Breakpoints

When you need to inspect more carefully what's happening in your code, you can set breakpoints in your browser's developer tools:

19. Go to the "Sources" tab in your developer tools.

20. Navigate to the source file you want to debug.
21. Click on the line number where you want to set the breakpoint.

When your code execution reaches that line, it will pause, and you can inspect the current state, variable values, and the call stack.

Debugging in Visual Studio Code

If you're using Visual Studio Code, you can debug your Vue.js project directly within the editor.

22. **Install the Debugger for Chrome Extension:**
    - Go to the extensions marketplace and search for "Debugger for Chrome".
    - Install the extension.
23. **Configure the Debugger:**
    - Add a .vscode/launch.json file in your project's root directory with the following configuration:

```
{
  "version": "0.2.0",
  "configurations": [
    {
      "type": "chrome",
      "request": "launch",
      "name": "Launch Chrome against localhost",
      "url": "http://localhost:8080",
      "webRoot": "${workspaceFolder}/src"
    }
  ]
}
```

24. **Debug Your Application:**
    - Start your local development server: npm run serve
    - Open the "Run" view in Visual Studio Code and start the debug configuration.

- Visual Studio Code will launch a new Chrome window and attach the debugger.

Handling Common Issues

Port Conflicts

If `http://localhost:8080/` is already in use, you can specify a different port in the `vue.config.js`:

```
// vue.config.js
module.exports = {
  devServer: {
    port: 3000,
  },
};
```

Run `npm run serve` again, and your application should now be available at `http://localhost:3000/`.

By using these tools and techniques, you can efficiently run and debug your Vue.js applications, ensuring you catch errors early and maintain a smooth development workflow.

3. Understanding Vue Components

3.1 Introduction to Vue Components

Vue.js is designed around the concept of components, offering a modular and reusable approach to building web interfaces. In this chapter, we will delve into the core of Vue components, understanding their structure, usage, and the benefits they bring to modern web development.

What are Vue Components?

At its core, a Vue component is a Vue instance with predefined options. They allow developers to encapsulate reusable parts of an interface into standalone, maintainable units. This modular approach helps manage complex interfaces as each component can be independently developed and tested.

Basic Vue Component Example

Consider an example where we need a button and a message. Instead of writing the same code repeatedly, we can create a component for it:

```
<div id="app">
  <message-button></message-button>
</div>

<script>
Vue.component('message-button', {
  template: '<button @click="showMessage">Click me</button>
',
  methods: {
    showMessage() {
      alert('Hello from Vue Component!');
    }
  }
})

new Vue({
  el: '#app'
})
</script>
```

In this example, we defined a `message-button` component that includes a button and a method to show a message when the button is clicked. The component is then used inside the main Vue instance.

The Benefits of Using Vue Components

1. **Reusability**: Components can be reused across multiple parts of the application, reducing code duplication.
2. **Maintainability**: Isolating functionality into components makes the application easier to manage, test, and debug.
3. **Encapsulation**: Components encapsulate their functionality and styles, reducing the risk of style leakage and conflicts.

Component-based Architecture

Using components, you can construct a complex user interface by combining smaller, simpler pieces. For example:

```
<div id="app">
  <navbar></navbar>
  <sidebar></sidebar>
  <content></content>
</div>

<script>
Vue.component('navbar', {
  template: '<div class="navbar">Navigation Bar</div>'
});

Vue.component('sidebar', {
  template: '<div class="sidebar">Sidebar Content</div>'
});

Vue.component('content', {
  template: '<div class="content">Main Content Area</div>'
});

new Vue({
  el: '#app'
});
</script>
```

Each part of the interface (navbar, sidebar, content) is defined as a separate component, making the code easy to understand and modify.

Dynamic Components

Vue also supports dynamic components, which enable the component being displayed to change according to application state:

```
<div id="app">
  <component :is="currentComponent"></component>
  <button @click="switchComponent">Switch Component</button>
</div>

<script>
Vue.component('component-a', {
  template: '<div>Component A</div>'
});

Vue.component('component-b', {
  template: '<div>Component B</div>'
});

new Vue({
  el: '#app',
  data: {
    currentComponent: 'component-a'
  },
  methods: {
    switchComponent() {
      this.currentComponent = this.currentComponent === 'component-a' ? 'component-b' : 'component-a';
    }
  }
});
</script>
```

In this example, the `component` element's `is` attribute determines which component to render based on the value of `currentComponent`.

Summary

Vue components are the building blocks of a Vue application, offering a modular, reusable, and maintainable approach to building web interfaces. They can encapsulate HTML, CSS, and JavaScript, breaking down complex UIs into manageable pieces. As you continue reading this chapter, you will explore more advanced topics about component registration, communication, and encapsulation in Vue.js.

3.2 Component Registration and Usage

Vue components are the building blocks of modern web applications, allowing developers to break the user interface into reusable and modular parts. In this subchapter, we will explore the process of registering and using Vue components both locally and globally.

Local Registration

In Vue, components can be registered locally within a single Vue instance. This is particularly useful when the component is only relevant to a specific part of your application. Local registration ensures that the component will only be available within the scope of the component in which it's registered.

To register a component locally, you need to include it in the `components` option of your Vue instance. Here's an example:

```
// MyComponent.vue
<template>
  <div>
    <p>This is a local component!</p>
  </div>
</template>

<script>
export default {
  name: 'MyComponent'
}
</script>

// ParentComponent.vue
<template>
  <div>
    <MyComponent />
  </div>
</template>

<script>
import MyComponent from './MyComponent.vue'

export default {
  name: 'ParentComponent',
  components: {
    MyComponent
  }
}
</script>
```

In this example, `MyComponent` is registered locally in `ParentComponent`. You can then use the `<MyComponent />` element within the template of `ParentComponent`.

Global Registration

If a component will be used across multiple parts of the application, it might make sense to register it globally. Global registration ensures that the component is available throughout the entire application without needing to import and register it in each component.

To register a component globally, use the `Vue.component` method:

```vue
// MyComponent.vue
<template>
  <div>
    <p>This is a global component!</p>
  </div>
</template>

<script>
export default {
  name: 'MyComponent'
}
</script>

// main.js
import Vue from 'vue'
import MyComponent from './components/MyComponent.vue'

Vue.component('MyComponent', MyComponent)

new Vue({
  el: '#app'
})
```

In this example, MyComponent is registered globally in `main.js` using `Vue.component`. Once registered globally, you can use `<MyComponent />` in any template within the Vue instance.

Using Registered Components

Once a component is registered, whether locally or globally, it can be used in the template by placing its custom element tag. Vue components follow kebab-case naming convention in templates.

For example:

```
<!-- Using the locally registered component -->
<ParentComponent>
  <my-component></my-component>
</ParentComponent>

<!-- Using the globally registered component -->
<my-component></my-component>
```

Vue uses custom elements in the form of kebab-case, regardless of how the component name is declared in JavaScript (PascalCase or camelCase).

Common Pitfalls and Best Practices

1. **Consistency in Naming**: Always use clear and consistent naming for your components. Prefer using PascalCase for component filenames and names.

2. **Local vs. Global Registration**: Think carefully about the scope in which a component will be used. Use local registration when the component is specific to a particular context and global registration when the component is reused throughout the application.

3. **Avoiding Component Bloat**: Don't overuse global components. Too many global components can lead to a bloated application. Use local registration when possible to keep your components organized.

4. **Component Naming Conventions**: When using multiple words in a component name, separate the words with hyphens (kebab-case). For example, `<my-component />`.

In conclusion, understanding how to properly register and use Vue components is crucial for building scalable and maintainable applications. The choice between local and global registration should be made based on the component's usage scope within your application.

By following best practices and avoiding common pitfalls, you will be better equipped to build modular and reusable Vue components, simplifying the development process and improving code maintenance.

3.3 Single File Components

Vue has revolutionized web development by encouraging the creation of small, reusable, and self-contained units of functionality called components. When putting these ideas into practice, the proper handling and structuring of these components become crucial for building maintainable applications. One of the most powerful features Vue offers is Single File Components (SFCs).

What is a Single File Component?

A Single File Component (SFC) is a Vue component written in a .vue file. Each .vue file encapsulates the HTML, JavaScript, and CSS of the component. This format promotes a modular approach to development by keeping all related parts of a component within the same file.

Here's the structure of a typical SFC:

```vue
<template>
  <div class="my-component">
    <h1>{{ title }}</h1>
    <p>{{ content }}</p>
    <button @click="updateContent">Update Content</button>
  </div>
</template>

<script>
export default {
  name: 'MyComponent',
  data() {
    return {
      title: 'Hello, Vue!',
      content: 'This is a Single File Component.'
    };
  },
  methods: {
    updateContent() {
      this.content = 'Content updated!';
    }
  }
};
</script>

<style scoped>
.my-component {
  text-align: center;
}
</style>
```

Components of a Single File Component

1. Template Section

The `<template>` section contains the HTML markup of the component. It is where you define the structure of your component's UI.

```
<template>
  <div class="example-component">
    <h2>{{ message }}</h2>
  </div>
</template>
```

In the above example, the `<template>` tag contains the HTML that will be rendered when the component is used. The `{{ message }}` mustache syntax is a placeholder for dynamic content.

2. Script Section

The `<script>` section includes the JavaScript logic of the component, such as data, methods, lifecycle hooks, and more.

```
<script>
export default {
  name: 'ExampleComponent',
  data() {
    return {
      message: 'This is an example component'
    };
  }
};
</script>
```

Here, the script defines a new component called `ExampleComponent` and initializes a data property `message`. The `export default` syntax is used to export the component object, making it possible to import and use it in other parts of the application.

3. Style Section

The `<style>` section is where the CSS is written to style the component. By default, styles are global, but you can scope styles to the component to avoid conflicts.

```
<style scoped>
.example-component {
  color: blue;
}
</style>
```

Using the scoped attribute ensures that the styles are applied only to this component, preventing potential clashes with other styles in the application.

The Benefits of Single File Components

1. **Encapsulation**: SFCs encapsulate HTML, JavaScript, and CSS in a single file, which makes components easier to manage and reason about.

2. **Reusability**: Components can be reused across different parts of the application, promoting DRY (Don't Repeat Yourself) principles.

3. **Better Tooling**: With SFCs, you can leverage Vue CLI and other tools to offer features like hot module replacement, code splitting, and linting.

4. **Modularity**: SFCs encourage a modular architecture, making it easier to maintain and scale applications.

Best Practices for Single File Components

- **Structure Components Properly**: Ensure that each component encapsulates only one piece of functionality.

- **Use Scoped Styles**: When necessary, use scoped styles to limit CSS to individual components, avoiding global style conflicts.

- **Name Components Appropriately**: Use clear and descriptive names for your components.

- **Split Large Templates and Scripts**: If a component becomes too large, consider splitting parts of the template or script into mixins or slots for better maintainability.

Example of Importing and Using a Single File Component

Here's how you can include and use an SFC in another Vue component:

```
// Import the component
import MyComponent from './components/MyComponent.vue';

export default {
  name: 'App',
  components: {
    MyComponent
  }
};

<template>
  <div id="app">
    <MyComponent />
  </div>
</template>
```

In this example, MyComponent is imported into the App component and then used within its template. This allows for easy composition and organization of different parts of your Vue application.

Additional Resources

For a deeper dive into SFCs and their capabilities, check out the official Vue documentation: https://vuejs.org/v2/guide/single-file-components.html

In conclusion, Single File Components offer a powerful and effective way of writing Vue components by consolidating all relevant parts into a cohesive, readable unit. As you continue building applications with Vue.js, leveraging SFCs will make your work more modular, maintainable, and scalable.

3.4 Communication Between Components

In modern web applications, components rarely live in isolation. Effective communication between components is crucial for building dynamic and interactive applications. In Vue.js, there are several patterns and techniques to facilitate communication between components, each serving different purposes and suiting various scenarios. This subchapter explores these techniques, including props, custom events, and more advanced methods like event buses and Vuex.

Props

Props (short for properties) are the primary way to pass data from a parent component to a child component in Vue.js. Props are customized attributes that enable you to pass dynamic data from one component to another.

Example

Let's assume you have a parent component `ParentComponent.vue` and a child component `ChildComponent.vue`. The parent component can pass data to the child component using props.

ParentComponent.vue:

```
<template>
  <div>
    <ChildComponent :message="parentMessage" />
  </div>
</template>

<script>
import ChildComponent from './ChildComponent.vue';

export default {
  components: {
    ChildComponent
  },
  data() {
    return {
      parentMessage: 'Hello from Parent!'
    };
  }
};
</script>
```

ChildComponent.vue:

```
<template>
  <div>
    {{ message }}
  </div>
</template>

<script>
export default {
  props: {
    message: {
      type: String,
      required: true
    }
  }
};
</script>
```

Custom Events

Custom events allow child components to communicate with their parent components. A child component can emit an event, and the parent component can listen for that event and respond accordingly.

Example

Let's enhance the previous example by allowing the child component to send a message back to the parent.

ParentComponent.vue:

```
<template>
  <div>
    <ChildComponent @childEvent="handleChildEvent" />
  </div>
</template>

<script>
import ChildComponent from './ChildComponent.vue';

export default {
  components: {
    ChildComponent
  },
  methods: {
    handleChildEvent(message) {
      console.log('Received from child:', message);
    }
  }
};
</script>
```

ChildComponent.vue:

```
<template>
  <div>
    <button @click="sendMessage">Send Message to Parent</button>
  </div>
</template>

<script>
export default {
  methods: {
    sendMessage() {
      this.$emit('childEvent', 'Hello from Child!');
    }
  }
};
</script>
```

Event Bus

For more complex applications where events must be shared between components that do not have a parent-child relationship, an event bus can be a useful pattern. An event bus is simply a new Vue instance that can be used to facilitate communication.

Example

First, create a new file for the event bus:

eventBus.js:

```
import Vue from 'vue';
export const EventBus = new Vue();
```

Use the event bus in components to emit and listen for events.

ComponentA.vue:

```
<template>
  <button @click="sendEvent">Send Event</button>
</template>

<script>
import { EventBus } from './eventBus.js';

export default {
  methods: {
    sendEvent() {
      EventBus.$emit('customEvent', 'Hello from ComponentA!');
    }
  }
};
</script>
```

ComponentB.vue:

```
<template>
  <div>
    {{ message }}
  </div>
</template>

<script>
import { EventBus } from './eventBus.js';

export default {
  data() {
    return {
      message: ''
    };
  },
  created() {
    EventBus.$on('customEvent', (msg) => {
      this.message = msg;
    });
  }
};
</script>
```

Vuex

When your application grows and you need a more robust state management solution, Vuex is the recommended library. Vuex provides a centralized store for all components in an application, enabling you to manage the state globally.

Example

First, set up a Vuex store.

store.js:

```js
import Vue from 'vue';
import Vuex from 'vuex';

Vue.use(Vuex);

export default new Vuex.Store({
  state: {
    message: 'Hello from Vuex Store!'
  },
  mutations: {
    updateMessage(state, newMessage) {
      state.message = newMessage;
    }
  },
  actions: {
    setMessage({ commit }, newMessage) {
      commit('updateMessage', newMessage);
    }
  }
});
```

Use Vuex in a component to get and set the state.

ComponentC.vue:

```
<template>
  <div>
    {{ message }}
    <button @click="updateMessage">Update Message</button>
  </div>
</template>

<script>
import { mapState, mapActions } from 'vuex';

export default {
  computed: {
    ...mapState(['message'])
  },
  methods: {
    ...mapActions(['setMessage']),
    updateMessage() {
      this.setMessage('Updated Hello from Vuex!');
    }
  }
};
</script>
```

In this subchapter, we've explored various methods for communication between Vue components, including props, custom events, event buses, and Vuex. Each method has its place and can be chosen based on the architectural needs of your application.

4. State Management with Vuex

4.1 Introduction to Vuex

State management is a crucial aspect of modern web applications, especially as they grow in size and complexity. Vuex is the official state management library for Vue.js applications, designed to handle the shared state across components efficiently. In this subchapter, we'll introduce Vuex and explain its core concepts to help you understand how it can revolutionize your Vue.js development experience.

What is Vuex?

Vuex is a state management pattern and library for Vue.js applications. It serves as a centralized store for all the components in an application, enabling a single source of truth. This makes debugging and testing easier since the state is managed in a predictable manner. Here's a simple analogy: think of Vuex as a local storage system where all components can store and retrieve shared data without prop drilling or event emission complications.

When to Use Vuex

While Vue's reactive data properties can handle local component state efficiently, Vuex becomes invaluable when:

- Your application has a significant amount of shared state.
- Multiple components need to communicate and share data.
- You want to keep your codebase scalable and maintainable.
- You need to debug state changes efficiently.

Installing Vuex

First, you need to install Vuex. If you are using Vue CLI, you can add Vuex by running:

```
vue add vuex
```

Alternatively, you can install it using npm or yarn:

```
npm install vuex
```

or

```
yarn add vuex
```

Initializing Vuex in a Vue Application

To initialize Vuex in your Vue application, you'll need to create a store. A store is where your state, mutations, actions, and getters reside. Here's how to set up a basic Vuex store.

Create a file named `store.js` in your project's `src` directory:

```js
import Vue from 'vue'
import Vuex from 'vuex'

Vue.use(Vuex)

export default new Vuex.Store({
  state: {
    count: 0
  },
  mutations: {
    increment(state) {
      state.count++
    }
  },
  actions: {
    increment({ commit }) {
      commit('increment')
    }
  },
  getters: {
    count: state => state.count
  }
})
```

Then, include the store in your Vue instance, usually found in `main.js`:

```js
import Vue from 'vue'
import App from './App.vue'
import store from './store'

Vue.config.productionTip = false

new Vue({
  store,
  render: h => h(App)
}).$mount('#app')
```

Core Concepts of Vuex

1. **State**: This is the single source of truth for your application's data. All components use this centralized state rather than managing their own local state.

2. **Getters**: These are like computed properties for stores. They allow you to retrieve and format the state's data.

3. **Mutations**: These are the only way to change the state. They must be synchronous to allow proper state tracking and debugging.

4. **Actions**: These are similar to mutations, but they can be asynchronous. Actions commit mutations after finishing asynchronous operations like API calls.

5. **Modules**: These allow you to split your store into multiple modules, each with its own state, mutations, actions, and getters. This helps in keeping your codebase organized and manageable.

Basic Usage Example

Here is a straightforward example demonstrating how to use Vuex in a Vue component:

```
<template>
  <div>
    <p>{{ count }}</p>
    <button @click="increment">Increment</button>
  </div>
</template>

<script>
import { mapGetters, mapActions } from 'vuex'

export default {
  computed: {
    ...mapGetters(['count'])
  },
  methods: {
    ...mapActions(['increment'])
  }
}
</script>
```

In this example, the `count` is retrieved from the Vuex store using a getter, and the `increment` method is an action that commits a mutation to increment the count.

Conclusion

Vuex provides a robust solution for state management in Vue.js applications, simplifying the complexity of handling state across your application. By mastering Vuex, you can build scalable and maintainable applications with ease. In the next subchapters, we will delve deeper into state, getters, mutations, actions, and modules to help you harness the full power of Vuex.

4.2 State, Getters, and Mutations

When managing state in more complex Vue applications, Vuex becomes an indispensable tool. In this subchapter, we will delve deeper into the core concepts of Vuex: State, Getters, and Mutations. Understanding these concepts is crucial for effectively managing and manipulating the application's state.

State

The state in Vuex represents the single source of truth. Think of it as the central repository for all data that your Vue applications need to manage. You can access state directly from your components and make the state data reactive.

Defining State

To define state, you create a state object within the Vuex store. Here's an example of a simple Vuex state:

```
const store = new Vuex.Store({
  state: {
    count: 0,
    todos: [
      { id: 1, text: 'Learn Vuex', done: true },
      { id: 2, text: 'Build a Vuex app', done: false }
    ]
  }
});
```

Accessing State

Components can access the state using the `this.$store.state` property:

```
computed: {
  count() {
    return this.$store.state.count;
  },
  todos() {
    return this.$store.state.todos;
  }
}
```

Getters

Getters are the Vuex equivalent of computed properties for stores. They allow you to create derived state based on store state. Getters can be defined to encapsulate any necessary calculations or filtering criteria.

Defining Getters

Here's how you define getters in Vuex:

```
const store = new Vuex.Store({
  state: {
    todos: [
      { id: 1, text: 'Learn Vuex', done: true },
      { id: 2, text: 'Build a Vuex app', done: false }
    ]
  },
  getters: {
    doneTodos: (state) => {
      return state.todos.filter(todo => todo.done);
    },
    doneTodosCount: (state, getters) => {
      return getters.doneTodos.length;
    }
  }
});
```

Accessing Getters

You can access the getters from within Vue components using the `this.$store.getters` property:

```
computed: {
  doneTodos() {
    return this.$store.getters.doneTodos;
  },
  doneTodosCount() {
    return this.$store.getters.doneTodosCount;
  }
}
```

Mutations

Mutations are the only way to modify the state in Vuex. They are synchronous transactions that directly change the state in a predictable manner. Each mutation has a handler function and a type.

Defining Mutations

Here's an example of defining mutations in Vuex:

```
const store = new Vuex.Store({
  state: {
    count: 0
  },
  mutations: {
    increment(state) {
      state.count++;
    },
    decrement(state) {
      state.count--;
    },
    incrementBy(state, payload) {
      state.count += payload.amount;
    }
  }
});
```

Committing Mutations

To change the state, you need to commit a mutation from within your Vue components using this.$store.commit('mutationType'):

```
methods: {
  increment() {
    this.$store.commit('increment');
  },
  decrement() {
    this.$store.commit('decrement');
  },
  incrementBy(amount) {
    this.$store.commit('incrementBy', { amount });
  }
}
```

Best Practices

- **Centralize all state:** Centralizing the state in Vuex can greatly enhance the maintainability and debuggability of your application.

- **Use meaningful names for mutations:** Mutation types should be named carefully to clearly indicate their purpose.

- **Leverage getters for derived state:** Instead of duplicating the logic to derive state data, use getters effectively.

In summary, understanding and leveraging state, getters, and mutations are fundamental to mastering Vuex for state management in Vue applications. The next subchapter will delve into actions and modules, which will enable you to handle asynchronous tasks and further organize your store.

4.3 Actions and Modules

In the previous subchapter, we discussed the core concepts of state, getters, and mutations in Vuex. In this subchapter, we will dive into actions and modules, which are essential for enhancing the structure and scalability of your Vuex store. Actions help manage asynchronous operations, while modules allow you to break down your store into self-contained units.

Actions

While mutations must be synchronous, actions can be asynchronous. This makes actions the perfect place to perform tasks like API calls, timers, and other asynchronous operations. Unlike mutations, actions commit mutations rather than mutating the state directly.

Defining Actions

Actions are defined in the `actions` object of your Vuex store. Each action handler receives a context object, which exposes methods and properties on the store instance, such as `commit` and `state`.

```
// store.js
const store = new Vuex.Store({
  state: {
    count: 0
  },
  mutations: {
    increment(state, payload) {
      state.count += payload.amount;
    }
  },
  actions: {
    incrementAsync({ commit }, payload) {
      setTimeout(() => {
        commit('increment', payload);
      }, 1000);
    }
  }
});
```

In this example, the `incrementAsync` action waits for one second before committing the `increment` mutation.

Dispatching Actions

To dispatch an action from your Vue component, use the `dispatch` method.

```
// MyComponent.vue
<template>
  <button @click="incrementCounter">Increment Async</button>
</template>

<script>
export default {
  methods: {
    incrementCounter() {
      this.$store.dispatch('incrementAsync', { amount: 5 })
;
    }
  }
};
</script>
```

When the button is clicked, the `incrementCounter` method dispatches the `incrementAsync` action, which then commits the `increment` mutation after a delay.

Modules

As your application grows, managing a single Vuex store can become cumbersome. Vuex allows you to divide your store into modules. Each module contains its own state, mutations, actions, and getters, making your store more manageable and organized.

Defining Modules

Modules are defined as objects with the same properties as the root store. You can then register these modules in the root store.

```
// modules/counter.js
const counter = {
  state: () => ({
    count: 0
  }),
  mutations: {
    increment(state, payload) {
      state.count += payload.amount;
    }
  },
  actions: {
    incrementAsync({ commit }, payload) {
      setTimeout(() => {
        commit('increment', payload);
      }, 1000);
    }
  },
  getters: {
    doubleCount(state) {
      return state.count * 2;
    }
  }
};

export default counter;
```

Registering Modules

Register the module in the root Vuex store by using the `modules` option.

```
// store.js
import Vue from 'vue';
import Vuex from 'vuex';
import counter from './modules/counter';

Vue.use(Vuex);

const store = new Vuex.Store({
  modules: {
    counter
  }
});

export default store;
```

Accessing Module State

When using modules, you can access state, mutations, actions, and getters by their module namespace.

```
// MyComponent.vue
<template>
  <div>
    <p>{{ count }}</p>
    <p>{{ doubleCount }}</p>
    <button @click="incrementCounter">Increment Async</button>
  </div>
</template>

<script>
export default {
  computed: {
    count() {
      return this.$store.state.counter.count;
    },
    doubleCount() {
      return this.$store.getters['counter/doubleCount'];
    }
  },
  methods: {
    incrementCounter() {
      this.$store.dispatch('counter/incrementAsync', { amount: 5 });
    }
  }
};
</script>
```

In this example, `count` and `doubleCount` are accessed from the counter module, and the `incrementAsync` action is dispatched from the `counter` module as well.

By effectively using actions and modules, you can manage complexity and maintain scalable state management in your Vue.js applications. These concepts will enable you to build more robust and maintainable code, especially as your application grows.

4.4 Best Practices for State Management

State management is a crucial aspect of building scalable and maintainable applications with Vue.js and Vuex. Adopting best practices not only enhances the readability and maintainability of your code but also prevents common pitfalls and errors. In this subchapter, we'll explore key practices you should consider when managing state in your Vue applications.

Keep State Flat

A flat state structure is often easier to manage and understand than deeply nested state trees. Flatten your state whenever possible to avoid complex state mutations and getter functions.

Example:

```
// Avoid deeply nested state
const state = {
  user: {
    profile: {
      name: 'John Doe',
    },
  },
  settings: {
    theme: 'dark',
  },
};

// Prefer a flat state
const state = {
  userName: 'John Doe',
  theme: 'dark',
};
```

Modularize Your State

Using Vuex modules allows you to break down your state management into smaller, more manageable pieces. Each module can contain its own state, mutations, actions, and getters, making your store easier to read and maintain.

Example:

```js
// store/modules/user.js
const state = {
  name: 'John Doe',
};

const mutations = {
  SET_NAME(state, name) {
    state.name = name;
  },
};

const actions = {
  updateName({ commit }, name) {
    commit('SET_NAME', name);
  },
};

const getters = {
  userName: (state) => state.name,
};

export default {
  state,
  mutations,
  actions,
  getters,
};

// store/index.js
import Vue from 'vue';
import Vuex from 'vuex';
import userModule from './modules/user';

Vue.use(Vuex);

export default new Vuex.Store({
  modules: {
    user: userModule,
  },
});
```

Use Namespaces

Namespaces in Vuex modules help to avoid naming conflicts and make your code more explicit. By enabling namespaced mode, all your module's mutations, actions, and getters are automatically namespaced.

Example:

```
const userModule = {
  namespaced: true,
  state: {
    name: 'John Doe',
  },
  mutations: {
    SET_NAME(state, name) {
      state.name = name;
    },
  },
  actions: {
    updateName({ commit }, name) {
      commit('SET_NAME', name);
    },
  },
  getters: {
    userName: (state) => state.name,
  },
};

// Accessing namespaced module
store.dispatch('user/updateName', 'Jane Doe');
store.commit('user/SET_NAME', 'Jane Doe');
store.getters['user/userName'];
```

Use Mutations for State Changes

Always use mutations to modify the state. Directly altering the state in actions or components can cause unpredictable behavior and make it difficult to track state changes.

Example:

```js
// Correct way
const mutations = {
  SET_THEME(state, theme) {
    state.theme = theme;
  },
};

const actions = {
  updateTheme({ commit }, theme) {
    commit('SET_THEME', theme);
  },
};

// Mutate state only through mutations
store.dispatch('updateTheme', 'Light');
```

Separate API Calls from State Management

Keep your API calls and business logic separate from your Vuex state management. This ensures that your Vuex store remains a clean layer for managing state.

Example:

```js
// api.js
export const fetchUserData = () => {
  return fetch('https://jsonplaceholder.typicode.com/users/1')
    .then(response => response.json());
};

// actions.js
import { fetchUserData } from './api';

const actions = {
  async loadUserData({ commit }) {
    const data = await fetchUserData();
    commit('SET_USER_DATA', data);
  },
};

// mutations.js
const mutations = {
  SET_USER_DATA(state, userData) {
    state.userData = userData;
  },
};
```

Keep Getters Simple

Getters should be used for simple state derivations rather than complex logic. If you find yourself writing intricate getters, consider whether the derived state should be stored in a different way.

Example:

```
const getters = {
  userFullName: (state) => `${state.firstName} ${state.lastName}`,
};

// Avoid complex logic in getters
const getters = {
  // Complex getter (better to handle this elsewhere)
  userProfile: (state) => {
    if (state.userDetails) {
      return `${state.userDetails.firstName} ${state.userDetails.LastName}`;
    }
    return '';
  },
};
```

Use Action for Asynchronous Operations

Always perform asynchronous operations (like API calls) in actions, not in mutations or getters. Actions can commit mutations, which then change the state.

Example:

```
const actions = {
  async fetchUserProfile({ commit }) {
    try {
      const response = await fetch('https://jsonplaceholder.typicode.com/users/1');
      const data = await response.json();
      commit('SET_USER_PROFILE', data);
    } catch (error) {
      console.error('Failed to fetch user profile:', error);
    }
  },
};

const mutations = {
  SET_USER_PROFILE(state, profile) {
    state.profile = profile;
  },
};
```

Avoid Over-Using the Store

Not all data needs to be stored in Vuex. Store only the state that is shared across multiple components. Local component state can be managed within the component itself.

Example:

```
// In Vuex store (shared state)
const state = {
  theme: 'dark',
  user: {
    name: 'John Doe',
  },
};

// In component (local state)
data() {
  return {
    localCounter: 0,
  };
},
methods: {
  incrementCounter() {
    this.localCounter++;
  },
},
```

By following these best practices, you'll be able to build Vuex stores that are easier to understand, debug, and maintain. This will ultimately lead to more robust and scalable Vue.js applications.

5. Vue Router for Single Page Applications

5.1 Basics of Vue Router

Vue Router is the official router for Vue.js, designed to create single-page applications (SPAs) with ease. It integrates deeply with Vue.js and offers a seamless way to handle navigation and state management within your applications. In this subchapter, we will explore the core concepts of Vue Router, including basic setup, defining routes, and creating link navigation.

Setting Up Vue Router

To get started with Vue Router, you first need to install it. If you've created your Vue project using Vue CLI, you can add Vue Router using npm or yarn:

```
npm install vue-router
# or
yarn add vue-router
```

Once the package is installed, you need to configure it in your Vue application. This is typically done in your main JavaScript file (e.g., main.js):

```
import Vue from 'vue';
import App from './App.vue';
import VueRouter from 'vue-router';
import Home from './components/Home.vue';
import About from './components/About.vue';

Vue.config.productionTip = false;

Vue.use(VueRouter);

const routes = [
  { path: '/', component: Home },
  { path: '/about', component: About },
];

const router = new VueRouter({
  routes
});

new Vue({
  render: h => h(App),
  router
}).$mount('#app');
```

Defining Routes

In the example above, we've imported the necessary components (Home.vue and About.vue) and defined routes corresponding to these components. Each route is an object with a `path` and a `component`.

Example: Basic Routes Configuration

Here's a more detailed example of how you might define several routes:

```
const routes = [
  { path: '/', component: Home },
  { path: '/about', component: About },
  { path: '/contact', component: Contact },
  { path: '*', component: NotFound } // Catch-all for 404 Not Found
];
```

Navigating Between Routes

Vue Router offers several methods to navigate between routes programmatically or via direct user interaction.

Using `<router-link>`

The `<router-link>` component is used to create navigable links in your application. It renders a standard HTML `<a>` element that the router listens to:

```
<template>
  <div>
    <router-link to="/">Home</router-link>
    <router-link to="/about">About</router-link>
    <router-link to="/contact">Contact</router-link>
  </div>
</template>
```

Programmatic Navigation

You can also navigate programmatically using the `this.$router` object within your Vue component's methods:

```
methods: {
  goToAbout() {
    this.$router.push('/about');
  }
}
```

Router Modes

Vue Router comes with two modes: **Hash Mode** and **History Mode**.

- **Hash Mode** (default): Uses the URL hash for navigation (example.com/#/about). It's compatible with all browsers but affects the aesthetics of the URL.

- **History Mode**: Uses the HTML5 History API, resulting in clean URLs (example.com/about). This requires server-side configuration to handle fallback to index.html for SPA routes.

To enable History Mode, you can pass the mode option when creating the VueRouter instance:

```
const router = new VueRouter({
  mode: 'history',
  routes: [
    { path: '/', component: Home },
    { path: '/about', component: About }
  ]
});
```

Route Parameters

You can define dynamic segments in your routes, allowing for more dynamic applications. Dynamic segments are denoted with a colon (:) prefix in the path:

```
const routes = [
  { path: '/user/:id', component: User },
];
```

In your User component, you can access the id parameter via this.$route.params.id:

```
export default {
  computed: {
    userId() {
      return this.$route.params.id;
    }
  }
}
```

Conclusion

The basic setup and usage of Vue Router lay the foundation for creating sophisticated single-page applications. By understanding how to define routes, create links, and navigate programmatically, you can manage the flow and structure of your application easily. In the subsequent sections, we'll delve deeper into advanced techniques such as dynamic routing, navigation guards, and lazy loading, which further enhance the functionality and performance of your Vue applications.

5.2 Dynamic Routing

Dynamic routing in Vue Router allows you to create routes with dynamic segments that can match multiple URLs. This is useful for creating URLs that can contain variable data, such as identifiers for specific resources or user profiles. In this subchapter, we will explore how to set up dynamic routes, access route parameters, and create nested dynamic routes for more complex applications.

Setting Up Dynamic Routes

To define a dynamic route, you use a colon (:) before the dynamic segment of your path. For instance, to create a user detail route where the user ID is a variable, you could set up the route as follows:

```
const routes = [
  {
    path: '/user/:id',
    component: UserDetail
  }
];
```

In this route, `:id` is a dynamic segment that can match any value. When a user navigates to `http://example.com/user/123`, the URL will match this route, and the value `123` will be available as a parameter.

Accessing Route Parameters

You can access dynamic route parameters in your component using the `$route` object. For example, inside the `UserDetail` component, you can fetch the `id` parameter:

```js
export default {
  mounted() {
    console.log(this.$route.params.id);
  }
};
```

In a real-world scenario, you might use this parameter to fetch additional data from an API:

```js
export default {
  data() {
    return {
      user: null
    };
  },
  async mounted() {
    const userId = this.$route.params.id;
    const response = await fetch(`http://api.example.com/users/${userId}`);
    this.user = await response.json();
  }
};
```

Nested Dynamic Routes

Sometimes, you may need more than one level of dynamic routing. For example, if you have a user profile route and need routes for the user's posts or settings, you can create nested routes with dynamic segments:

```
const routes = [
  {
    path: '/user/:id',
    component: UserDetail,
    children: [
      {
        path: 'posts',
        component: UserPosts
      },
      {
        path: 'settings',
        component: UserSettings
      }
    ]
  }
];
```

In this example, navigating to http://example.com/user/123/posts will render the UserDetail component and the UserPosts component inside it.

Programmatic Navigation

You can also navigate to dynamic routes programmatically using the this.$router.push method. This is useful if you want to redirect a user based on some conditions. Here's a quick example:

```
methods: {
  goToUser(userId) {
    this.$router.push(`/user/${userId}`);
  }
}
```

Catch-All Routes

For routes that serve as a fallback, you can use a catch-all route with an asterisk (*). This is especially useful for handling 404 errors:

```
const routes = [
  // other routes...
  {
    path: '*',
    component: NotFound
  }
];
```

This route will match any path that doesn't match the other defined routes and redirect users to a NotFound component.

Summary

Dynamic routing is a powerful feature that allows your Vue.js application to handle paths with variable segments, making your router more flexible and your URLs more meaningful. By understanding how to set up dynamic routes, access route parameters, and create nested dynamic routes, you can better manage complex navigation schemes in your single-page applications.

Next, we'll explore navigation guards, which provide hooks to control navigation based on various conditions. Let's dive into it in the next subchapter.

5.3 Navigation Guards

Navigation Guards are a powerful feature of Vue Router that allows you to control the navigation in your application. They help you manage tasks like authentication checks, fetching data before route navigation, or preventing navigation under certain conditions. This subchapter covers the different types of navigation guards available in Vue Router and how to use them effectively.

Global Guards

Global guards are defined on the `router` instance and apply to all routes. There are three types of global guards:

- `router.beforeEach`: Executes before every navigation.
- `router.beforeResolve`: Similar to `beforeEach` but is called after `beforeEnter` guards in route configurations.
- `router.afterEach`: Called after every navigation, but does not affect navigation itself.

Example of a `beforeEach` global guard:

```
const router = new VueRouter({
  routes: [
    { path: '/', component: Home },
    { path: '/about', component: About }
  ]
});

router.beforeEach((to, from, next) => {
  console.log('Navigation guard called');
  if (to.path !== '/about') {
    next();
  } else {
    next('/');
  }
});
```

In this example, if the user tries to navigate to the /about route, they are redirected to the / route.

Per-Route Guards

Per-route guards are defined directly in route configurations. These can be particularly useful when you want to apply guards to specific routes.

Example:

```
const routes = [
  {
    path: '/dashboard',
    component: Dashboard,
    beforeEnter: (to, from, next) => {
      if (store.state.isLoggedIn) {
        next();
      } else {
        next('/login');
      }
    }
  },
  { path: '/login', component: Login }
];
const router = new VueRouter({ routes });
```

In this case, the beforeEnter guard ensures that only authenticated users can access the /dashboard route by checking store.state.isLoggedIn.

In-Component Guards

In-component guards are defined inside your components. They are useful when you need more control over navigation within the component. There are three types of in-component guards:

- **beforeRouteEnter**: Called before the route that renders this component is confirmed.
- **beforeRouteUpdate**: Called when the route that renders this component is changing but the component is being reused.
- **beforeRouteLeave**: Called when the route that renders this component is about to be navigated away from.

Example using beforeRouteEnter:

```
const Dashboard = {
  template: '<div>Dashboard</div>',
  beforeRouteEnter (to, from, next) {
    if (store.state.isLoggedIn) {
      next();
    } else {
      next('/login');
    }
  }
};
```

In this example, the beforeRouteEnter guard checks if the user is logged in before allowing navigation to the Dashboard component.

Asynchronous Guards

Navigation guards can handle asynchronous operations. Simply use Promises or async/await within guards.

Example of using Promises:

```
router.beforeEach((to, from, next) => {
  fetch('http://example.com/api/check-auth')
    .then(response => response.json())
    .then(data => {
      if (data.isLoggedIn) {
        next();
      } else {
        next('/Login');
      }
    })
    .catch(() => {
      next('/login');
    });
});
```

In this example, the guard fetches data from an API to check if the user is authenticated before allowing navigation.

Using next Function

The next function in navigation guards can be used in several ways: - next(): Proceeds to the next hook or finalizes navigation. - next(false): Aborts the navigation. - next('/'): Redirects to a different route. - next(new Error('error message')): Throws an error, navigation can be caught with a centralized error handler.

Example:

```
router.beforeEach((to, from, next) => {
  if (to.path === '/secret') {
    if (!store.state.isLoggedIn) {
      next('/Login');
    } else {
      next();
    }
  } else {
    next();
  }
});
```

In this example, if the user attempts to navigate to the `/secret` route, they are redirected to the `/login` route if they are not logged in.

Summary

Navigation Guards are essential for managing navigation flow in complex applications. By understanding and utilizing global guards, per-route guards, in-component guards, and handling asynchronous operations, you can enhance the user experience and ensure robust route handling in your Vue.js application.

In the next subchapter, we will explore how to optimize your application using Lazy Loading Routes.

5.4 Lazy Loading Routes

Lazy loading is a concept that can significantly improve the performance of your Vue.js single-page application (SPA). Instead of loading all components upfront, lazy loading allows you to load components only when they are needed. This can reduce the initial bundle size and improve the loading time of your application.

What is Lazy Loading?

In the context of Vue Router, lazy loading refers to loading route components asynchronously. This means that the component will only be fetched from the server when the user navigates to the route that requires it. This can be particularly beneficial for large applications with many routes and components.

Benefits of Lazy Loading

- **Reduced Initial Load Time**: Only essential components are loaded initially, allowing the application to load faster.
- **Better User Experience**: Users can start interacting with the application sooner, as only the necessary part of the application is loaded.
- **Efficient Bandwidth Usage**: Unnecessary components are not loaded until required, conserving bandwidth.

How to Implement Lazy Loading

In Vue Router, you can implement lazy loading by using dynamic imports. Instead of importing components at the top of your script, you can use the `import` function to dynamically import components when they are needed.

Here's an example to illustrate how you can set this up:

```javascript
import Vue from 'vue';
import Router from 'vue-router';

Vue.use(Router);

const routes = [
  {
    path: '/home',
    name: 'Home',
    component: () => import('@/components/Home.vue'), // Lazy loaded
  },
  {
    path: '/about',
    name: 'About',
    component: () => import('@/components/About.vue'), // Lazy loaded
  },
  {
    path: '/contact',
    name: 'Contact',
    component: () => import('@/components/Contact.vue'), // Lazy loaded
  },
];

export default new Router({
  mode: 'history',
  routes,
});
```

In the example above, the Home, About, and `Contact` components are loaded only when a user navigates to their respective routes.

Handling Errors in Lazy Loading

Sometimes, dynamic imports can fail due to network issues or other unforeseen problems. Vue Router provides a way to handle such errors gracefully using the `errorCaptured` lifecycle hook.

```vue
<template>
  <div v-if="error">
    <p>Error loading component. Please try again later.</p>
  </div>
  <div v-else>
    <router-view></router-view>
  </div>
</template>

<script>
export default {
  data() {
    return {
      error: null,
    };
  },
  errorCaptured(err, vm, info) {
    this.error = err;
    console.error('Error captured in component:', info);
    return false;
  },
};
</script>
```

In this code snippet, if an error occurs while loading the component, an error message will be displayed to the user.

Preloading Dynamic Imports

While lazy loading reduces the initial load time, there are cases where you might want to preload certain dynamic imports. Vue Router doesn't provide native support for preloading, but you can achieve it using the `webpackPreload` magic comment.

```
{
  path: '/profile',
  name: 'Profile',
  component: () => import(/* webpackPreload: true */ '@/components/Profile.vue'), // Preloaded
}
```

This will hint to Webpack to preload the `Profile.vue` component, which can be useful for routes that you expect the user to navigate to shortly after the initial load.

Conclusion

Lazy loading routes is a powerful optimization technique that can improve the performance and user experience of your Vue.js single-page applications. By dynamically importing components only when they are needed, you can reduce the initial load time and make your application more efficient. Incorporate lazy loading into your routing strategy to enhance the overall performance of your Vue.js projects.

6. Vue Directives, Filters, and Mixins

6.1 Introduction to Vue Directives

Directives are one of the core features that make Vue.js stand out as a versatile and user-friendly front-end framework. This subchapter will introduce you to the concept of directives in Vue.js, explaining what they are, why they are important, and how to use them effectively.

What are Vue Directives?

Directives in Vue.js are special tokens in the markup that tell the library to do something to a DOM element. They are prefixed with v-, to indicate that they are special attributes provided by Vue. Essentially, directives are designed to encapsulate reusable DOM manipulations. They can be used to bind data to attributes, manage conditional rendering, handle event listening, and much more.

Why Use Directives?

Directives provide a declarative way to apply reactive behavior to your markup. Instead of imperatively attaching event listeners or modifying the DOM via JavaScript, directives allow you to express these behaviors directly in your HTML templates. This makes your code more readable, maintains a clean separation between structure and behavior, and leverages Vue's reactive system to efficiently update the DOM.

Basic Syntax of Vue Directives

The syntax for a directive in Vue is straightforward. A directive is denoted by `v-` followed by the directive name. For instance, to bind a piece of data to an element's text content, you can use the `v-bind` directive:

```
<div v-bind:title="message">
  Hover your mouse over me to see the dynamically bound title!
</div>
```

In this example, `message` is a piece of data in the Vue instance. The `v-bind` directive binds the value of `message` to the `title` attribute of the `div`.

Commonly Used Directives

Several built-in directives are frequently used when developing Vue.js applications. Here are some of the most commonly used ones:

v-bind

The `v-bind` directive is used to bind a data property to an attribute of an element. For example:

```
<img v-bind:src="imageUrl" alt="Description of image">
```

Here, the `src` attribute of the `img` tag is dynamically bound to the `imageUrl` data property.

v-model

The `v-model` directive creates a two-way binding on an input, select, or textarea element. This is particularly useful for handling form inputs. For instance:

```
<input v-model="email" placeholder="Enter your email">
```

In this case, whatever the user types into the input field is automatically reflected in the `email` data property.

v-for

The `v-for` directive is used for rendering a list of items based on an array. Example:

```
<ul>
  <li v-for="item in items" :key="item.id">
    {{ item.text }}
  </li>
</ul>
```

Here, each item in the `items` array is rendered as an `li` element inside the `ul`.

v-if

The `v-if` directive is used for conditional rendering. Example:

```
<p v-if="seen">Now you see me!</p>
```

In this example, the paragraph will be rendered only if the `seen` data property is `true`.

Directives vs. Methods

It's important to understand the distinction between using directives and methods for DOM manipulation. Where directives provide a declarative way to bind behavior within templates, methods offer an imperative approach. Generally, directives are preferable for cleaner, more maintainable templates, whereas methods might be used for complex or unique DOM manipulations that are not easily expressed with directives.

Summary

In summary, Vue directives are a powerful feature that allows you to declaratively bind data and manage DOM behavior within your templates. The use of directives like `v-bind`, `v-model`, `v-for`, and `v-if` can significantly simplify the development process by keeping your HTML clean and harnessing Vue's reactivity for efficient DOM updates. As we delve deeper into built-in and custom directives in the following subchapters, you'll see just how versatile and powerful Vue's directive system can be for modern web development.

In the next section, we will explore how to use these built-in directives with more detailed examples and best practices, solidifying your understanding and ability to use them effectively in your Vue.js applications.

6. Vue Directives, Filters, and Mixins

6.2 Using Built-in Directives

Vue.js offers a set of very useful built-in directives that help you manage DOM behavior in your applications. Whether you're conditionally rendering elements, iterating over data, or reacting to user input, Vue's built-in directives provide a powerful and flexible way to bind data to the DOM. Below, we will explore some of the most commonly used built-in directives.

v-bind

The `v-bind` directive is used to bind attributes to expressions. This allows you to dynamically set the value of an attribute.

```
<div v-bind:class="dynamicClass">Hello, Vue!</div>
```

In this example, the `class` attribute of the `div` element is dynamically bound to the `dynamicClass` property in the Vue instance.

```
new Vue({
  el: '#app',
  data: {
    dynamicClass: 'active'
  }
});
```

v-if, v-else-if, and v-else

These directives are used for conditional rendering. They allow you to display elements based on the truthiness of expressions.

```
<div v-if="showMessage">This is visible if showMessage is t
rue.</div>
<div v-else-if="showAlternateMessage">This is visible if sh
owAlternateMessage is true, but showMessage is false.</div>
<div v-else>This is visible if both showMessage and showAlt
ernateMessage are false.</div>

new Vue({
  el: '#app',
  data: {
    showMessage: true,
    showAlternateMessage: false
  }
});
```

v-for

The v-for directive is used for rendering lists of items by iterating over an array or an object.

```
<ul>
  <li v-for="item in items" :key="item.id">{{ item.text }}<
/li>
</ul>

new Vue({
  el: '#app',
  data: {
    items: [
      { id: 1, text: 'Learn Vue.js' },
      { id: 2, text: 'Build an app' },
      { id: 3, text: 'Deploy to production' }
    ]
  }
});
```

v-model

The v-model directive is used for two-way data binding on form input elements. It keeps the DOM in sync with the data in the Vue instance.

```
<input v-model="message" placeholder="Type a message">
<p>The message is: {{ message }}</p>
```

```
new Vue({
  el: '#app',
  data: {
    message: ''
  }
});
```

v-on

The v-on directive is used to listen for DOM events and execute methods when they occur.

```
<button v-on:click="showAlert">Click me</button>
new Vue({
  el: '#app',
  methods: {
    showAlert() {
      alert('Button clicked!');
    }
  }
});
```

Alternatively, you can use the shorthand @ for v-on.

```
<button @click="showAlert">Click me</button>
```

v-show

The v-show directive is another way to conditionally display elements. Unlike v-if, v-show still renders the element and uses CSS to toggle its visibility.

```
<div v-show="isVisible">This is conditionally visible.</div>
new Vue({
  el: '#app',
  data: {
    isVisible: true
  }
});
```

v-pre and v-cloak

The v-pre directive skips compilation for this element and all its children. This can be useful when you have static content or want to display raw template syntax.

```
<div v-pre>{{ rawContent }}</div>
```

The v-cloak directive is used to provide a way to keep some elements from being visible until Vue's compilation process is complete. Typically used in conjunction with CSS:

```
<style>
[v-cloak] {
  display: none;
}
</style>

<div v-cloak>{{ message }}</div>
```

Ensuring that your elements only become visible once Vue has finished compiling the template.

By effectively utilizing these built-in directives, you can create dynamic, efficient, and highly interactive web applications with Vue.js. Each directive serves a specific purpose, and they can be combined to create sophisticated user interfaces with minimal code.

6.3 Custom Directives in Vue.js

In addition to Vue's built-in directives, you can create custom directives to add reusable DOM manipulation capabilities tailored to your needs. Custom directives are useful when you need to perform low-level DOM operations or integrate with third-party libraries.

Creating a Custom Directive

To create a custom directive, use the `Vue.directive()` method. This method takes two arguments: a name (without the `v-` prefix) and an options object to define the lifecycle hooks.

Example: `v-focus` Directive

Let's create a simple custom directive called `v-focus` that automatically focuses on the input element when the component is mounted.

First, register the directive globally:

```
Vue.directive('focus', {
  inserted: function (el) {
    el.focus();
  }
});
```

To use the custom directive, simply add it to an input element in your template:

```
<template>
  <input v-focus />
</template>
```

This directive will automatically focus the input element when it is inserted into the DOM.

Local Registration of Custom Directives

Custom directives can also be registered locally within a Vue component. This is useful when the directive is specific to a component and doesn't need to be used globally.

```
export default {
  directives: {
    focus: {
      inserted(el) {
        el.focus();
      }
    }
  },
  template: `<input v-focus />`
};
```

Directive Lifecycle Hooks

Custom directives provide several lifecycle hooks that you can use to manage the directive's behavior:

- `bind`: Called once when the directive is bound to the element.
- `inserted`: Called when the bound element has been inserted into its parent node.
- `update`: Called when the component's VNode is updated, but before its children have been updated.
- `componentUpdated`: Called after the component's VNode and its children have been updated.
- `unbind`: Called once when the directive is unbound from the element.

Here's an example using these hooks to create a `v-resize` directive that handles window resizing:

```js
Vue.directive('resize', {
  bind(el, binding) {
    el.onResize = () => {
      binding.value();
    };
    window.addEventListener('resize', el.onResize);
  },
  unbind(el) {
    window.removeEventListener('resize', el.onResize);
  }
});
```

In your template, you can bind a method to this directive:

```html
<template>
  <div v-resize="onResize">Resize the window and check the console</div>
</template>

<script>
export default {
  methods: {
    onResize() {
      console.log('Window resized!');
    }
  }
};
</script>
```

Passing Values and Arguments to Directives

You can pass arguments and modifiers to custom directives, just like with built-in directives.

Example: `v-color` Directive

Let's create a custom directive `v-color` to change an element's color based on a passed value.

```
Vue.directive('color', {
  bind(el, binding) {
    el.style.color = binding.value;
  }
});
```

To use this directive:

```
<template>
  <div v-color="'blue'">This text will be blue</div>
</template>
```

To add an argument, modify the directive:

```
Vue.directive('color', {
  bind(el, binding) {
    el.style[binding.arg] = binding.value;
  }
});
```

Then use it in your template:

```
<template>
  <div v-color:background-color="'yellow'">This background color will be yellow</div>
</template>
```

Real-World Example: `v-tooltip` Directive

Creating a tooltip directive involves more complex DOM manipulation and integration with CSS for styling.

First, define the directive:

```js
Vue.directive('tooltip', {
  bind(el, binding) {
    let tooltipEl = document.createElement('div');
    tooltipEl.className = 'tooltip';
    tooltipEl.textContent = binding.value;
    el.appendChild(tooltipEl);

    el.onmouseenter = function () {
      tooltipEl.style.display = 'block';
    };

    el.onmouseleave = function () {
      tooltipEl.style.display = 'none';
    };
  },
  unbind(el) {
    el.onmouseenter = null;
    el.onmouseleave = null;
    if (el.querySelector('.tooltip')) {
      el.removeChild(el.querySelector('.tooltip'));
    }
  }
});
```

Add some CSS for the tooltip:

```css
.tooltip {
  display: none;
  position: absolute;
  background: rgba(0, 0, 0, 0.7);
  color: white;
  padding: 5px;
  border-radius: 3px;
}
```

And use the directive in your template:

```html
<template>
  <button v-tooltip="'Click me for more info.'">Hover me</button>
</template>
```

Conclusion

Custom directives in Vue.js provide a powerful way to extend the functionality of your Vue applications. By using custom directives, you can encapsulate and reuse complex DOM manipulations, offering a more polished and maintainable codebase.

6.4 Filters and Mixins: Enhancing Reusability

In Vue.js, reusability and modularity are crucial for building maintainable and scalable applications. Two powerful features, Filters and Mixins, facilitate this by allowing you to encapsulate and share logic across components. This subchapter will explore how to leverage these features to enhance your development workflow.

Filters: Transforming Data

Filters in Vue.js are methods that are used to format or transform the output of data in your templates. They are primarily used in text interpolation and `v-bind` expressions.

Using Filters

Filters are defined in the `filters` option of a Vue instance or a component. Here is a basic example:

```
new Vue({
  el: '#app',
  data: {
    price: 1234.56
  },
  filters: {
    currency(value) {
      return `$${value.toFixed(2)}`;
    }
  }
});
```

In the template, you can use this filter as follows:

```
<div id="app">
  <p>{{ price | currency }}</p>
</div>
```

Output:

```
$1234.56
```

Chaining Filters

Filters can also be chained, allowing you to apply multiple transformations. Here's an example of chaining a currency filter with an uppercase filter:

```
new Vue({
  el: '#app',
  data: {
    price: 1234.56
  },
  filters: {
    currency(value) {
      return `$${value.toFixed(2)}`;
    },
    uppercase(value) {
      return value.toUpperCase();
    }
  }
});
```

In the template:

```
<div id="app">
  <p>{{ price | currency | uppercase }}</p>
</div>
```

Output:

```
$1234.56
```

Mixins: Reusing Code Across Components

Mixins are a flexible way to distribute reusable functionality for Vue components. A mixin object can contain any component options, and when a component uses a mixin, all options in the mixin will be mixed into the component's own options.

Defining a Mixin

Let's create a mixin that adds a method to greet the user.

```js
const myMixin = {
  data() {
    return {
      user: 'John Doe'
    };
  },
  methods: {
    greet() {
      console.log(`Hello, ${this.user}!`);
    }
  }
};
```

Using a Mixin in a Component

You can use this mixin in a component like so:

```js
Vue.component('greet-user', {
  mixins: [myMixin],
  template: '<button @click="greet">Greet User</button>'
});

new Vue({
  el: '#app'
});
```

In the template:

```html
<div id="app">
  <greet-user></greet-user>
</div>
```

When you click the button, it will log:

```
Hello, John Doe!
```

Global Mixins

You can also register a global mixin that affects all Vue components. Use this approach with caution as it will apply to every component in your application and might have unintended side effects.

```
Vue.mixin({
  created() {
    console.log('Global Mixin - Created Hook');
  }
});

new Vue({
  el: '#app',
  template: '<div>Check the console for mixin messages.</div
v>'
});
```

Lifecycle Hooks in Mixins

Mixins can include lifecycle hooks, which are called at the same stage as component lifecycle hooks. If both a mixin and the component define a lifecycle hook, both hooks will be called. The mixin hook will be called first.

```
const lifecycleMixin = {
  created() {
    console.log('Mixin Created Hook');
  }
};

Vue.component('Lifecycle-demo', {
  mixins: [lifecycleMixin],
  created() {
    console.log('Component Created Hook');
  },
  template: '<div>Open the console to see the logs.</div>'
});

new Vue({
  el: '#app'
});
```

When the component is instantiated, it will log:

```
Mixin Created Hook
Component Created Hook
```

In conclusion, filters and mixins are essential tools for enhancing reusability in Vue.js applications. Filters help transform data in your templates, while mixins allow you to share reusable logic across multiple components. Utilize these features to write cleaner, more maintainable code.

7. Handling Forms and User Input in Vue

7.1. Introduction to Forms in Vue

Forms are a fundamental aspect of web development, providing a method for users to interact with an application by inputting and submitting data. In Vue.js, handling forms and user input is accomplished through a combination of data binding and built-in directives, making it both simple and powerful. This subchapter will introduce you to the key concepts and tools you need to handle forms effectively in Vue.js.

Two-Way Data Binding with `v-model`

One of the standout features of Vue.js is its declarative syntax, and the `v-model` directive is a prime example of this. `v-model` creates a two-way binding on form inputs, seamlessly reflecting input values in the component's data properties.

Here's a basic example to illustrate how `v-model` works:

```
<div id="app">
  <input v-model="message" placeholder="Enter a message">
  <p>{{ message }}</p>
</div>

<script>
new Vue({
  el: '#app',
  data: {
    message: ''
  }
})
</script>
```

In this example, any text entered in the input field will automatically update the `message` property in the Vue instance, and any changes to `message` will update the value shown in the input field.

Binding Different Input Types

Vue.js supports binding for a variety of input types like text, checkbox, radio buttons, and more. Here's how you can handle different types of inputs:

Text Inputs

```
<input v-model="username" placeholder="Enter your username">
```

Checkbox

```
<input type="checkbox" v-model="agreeToTerms"> I agree to the terms and conditions
```

Radio Buttons

```
<input type="radio" v-model="gender" value="male"> Male
<input type="radio" v-model="gender" value="female"> Female
```

Select Dropdown

```
<select v-model="selectedOption">
  <option disabled value="">Please select one</option>
  <option>A</option>
  <option>B</option>
  <option>C</option>
</select>
```

Modifiers for `v-model`

Vue.js also provides a set of useful modifiers that you can apply to v-model. These modifiers enhance the standard functionality of v-model, making it more adaptable to specific needs.

.lazy Modifier

The `.lazy` modifier updates the data binding only after the `change` event:

```
<input v-model.lazy="message" placeholder="Enter a message">
```

.number Modifier

The `.number` modifier automatically converts user input to a number if possible:

```
<input v-model.number="age" type="number" placeholder="Enter your age">
```

.trim Modifier

The `.trim` modifier automatically trims whitespace from the input:

```
<input v-model.trim="name" placeholder="Enter your name">
```

Event Handling

Vue's event handling system can be easily integrated with form elements to handle user input more robustly. The `v-on` directive (or `@` shorthand) is used to listen for DOM events:

```
<form @submit.prevent="onSubmit">
  <input v-model="username" placeholder="Enter your usernam
e">
  <button type="submit">Submit</button>
</form>

<script>
new Vue({
  el: '#app',
  data: {
    username: ''
  },
  methods: {
    onSubmit() {
      console.log('Form submitted with:', this.username);
    }
  }
})
</script>
```

In this example, the form submission is intercepted by Vue's event handler, allowing you to run custom logic when the form is submitted.

Summary

Understanding how to handle forms and user input in Vue.js is essential for building interactive applications. The `v-model` directive and its modifiers, along with Vue's event handling capabilities, offer a wide range of tools to manage form interactions efficiently and elegantly. In the following sections, we will dive deeper into binding user input with `v-model`, various form validation methods, and handling form submissions in Vue.js.

7.2. Binding User Input with v-model

Handling user input and efficiently managing forms is crucial in any web application. In Vue.js, the v-model directive provides a seamless way to bind form input elements to Vue instance data. This two-way data binding keeps your form inputs and your data in sync, simplifying the process of managing state changes and handling user inputs.

Understanding v-model

The v-model directive creates a binding between the value of a form input element and a variable in the Vue instance's data. This two-way data binding means that any changes to the input element's value will automatically be reflected in the variable, and any changes to the variable will be reflected in the input element's value.

Using v-model with Different Input Types

Let's explore how v-model can be used with different types of input elements.

Text Inputs

For a basic text input, v-model is straightforward. The directive binds an input element to a data property. Any changes made in the input are automatically reflected in the data property and vice versa.

```
<div id="app">
  <input type="text" v-model="username" placeholder="Enter your username">
  <p>Username: {{ username }}</p>
</div>

<script>
  new Vue({
    el: '#app',
    data: {
      username: ''
    }
  });
</script>
```

Checkbox Inputs

Checkboxes are equally simple to bind using `v-model`. For single checkboxes, `v-model` binds the checkbox's checked state to a Boolean.

```
<div id="app">
  <label>
    <input type="checkbox" v-model="isSubscribed">
    Subscribe to newsletter
  </label>
  <p>Subscribed: {{ isSubscribed }}</p>
</div>

<script>
  new Vue({
    el: '#app',
    data: {
      isSubscribed: false
    }
  });
</script>
```

For multiple checkboxes, `v-model` can bind the checked state to an array.

```
<div id="app">
  <label>
    <input type="checkbox" value="Option 1" v-model="selectedOptions">
    Option 1
  </label>
  <label>
    <input type="checkbox" value="Option 2" v-model="selectedOptions">
    Option 2
  </label>
  <p>Selected Options: {{ selectedOptions }}</p>
</div>

<script>
  new Vue({
    el: '#app',
    data: {
      selectedOptions: []
    }
  });
</script>
```

Radio Buttons

For radio buttons, where only one option can be selected from a group, v-model binds the selected value to a single variable.

```
<div id="app">
  <label>
    <input type="radio" value="Option A" v-model="picked">
    Option A
  </label>
  <label>
    <input type="radio" value="Option B" v-model="picked">
    Option B
  </label>
  <p>Picked: {{ picked }}</p>
</div>

<script>
  new Vue({
    el: '#app',
    data: {
      picked: ''
    }
  });
</script>
```

Select Dropdowns

Binding `v-model` with `<select>` elements works the same way. It can be used with both single and multiple selections.

```
<div id="app">
  <select v-model="selected">
    <option disabled value="">Please select one</option>
    <option>Option A</option>
    <option>Option B</option>
    <option>Option C</option>
  </select>
  <p>Selected: {{ selected }}</p>
</div>

<script>
  new Vue({
    el: '#app',
    data: {
      selected: ''
    }
  });
</script>
```

To allow multiple selections, you can use the `multiple` attribute and bind `v-model` to an array.

```
<div id="app">
  <select v-model="selectedMultiple" multiple>
    <option>Option A</option>
    <option>Option B</option>
    <option>Option C</option>
  </select>
  <p>Selected: {{ selectedMultiple }}</p>
</div>

<script>
  new Vue({
    el: '#app',
    data: {
      selectedMultiple: []
    }
  });
</script>
```

Modifiers

Vue provides various modifiers that allow you to customize `v-model` behavior. These modifiers include `.lazy`, `.number`, and `.trim`.

.lazy

By default, `v-model` synchronizes the input with the data property on the `input` event. Using the `.lazy` modifier, you can sync on the change event instead.

```
<div id="app">
  <input type="text" v-model.lazy="text" placeholder="Enter some text">
  <p>Text: {{ text }}</p>
</div>

<script>
  new Vue({
    el: '#app',
    data: {
      text: ''
    }
  });
</script>
```

.number

The `.number` modifier automatically converts the input value to a number.

```
<div id="app">
  <input type="text" v-model.number="age" placeholder="Enter your age">
  <p>Age: {{ age }}</p>
</div>

<script>
  new Vue({
    el: '#app',
    data: {
      age: ''
    }
  });
</script>
```

.trim

The `.trim` modifier trims whitespace from the input value.

```
<div id="app">
  <input type="text" v-model.trim="name" placeholder="Enter your name">
  <p>Name: {{ name }}</p>
</div>

<script>
  new Vue({
    el: '#app',
    data: {
      name: ''
    }
  });
</script>
```

Custom Input Components and v-model

For custom components, you need to implement `v-model` support. This is done using the `value` prop and emitting input events when the value changes.

```
<template>
  <div>
    <input :value="value" @input="$emit('input', $event.target.value)">
  </div>
</template>

<script>
export default {
  props: ['value']
};
</script>
```

Now you can use `v-model` with this custom component just like with any standard input element.

```
<div id="app">
  <custom-input v-model="customValue"></custom-input>
  <p>Custom Value: {{ customValue }}</p>
</div>

<script>
import CustomInput from './CustomInput.vue';

new Vue({
  el: '#app',
  components: {
    CustomInput
  },
  data: {
    customValue: ''
  }
});
</script>
```

By mastering the `v-model` directive, you can efficiently bind user inputs to your Vue instance data, enabling a seamless and dynamic user experience. Understanding how `v-model` works with different input types and how to use its modifiers will significantly improve the way you handle forms in your Vue applications.

7.3. Form Validation Methods

Form validation is a crucial aspect of web application development. It ensures that user-provided data meets the necessary criteria before being processed or stored. In this section, we will explore several methods to handle form validation in Vue.js.

Basic Validation with Computed Properties

Vue's computed properties offer a straightforward way to implement basic form validation. This method is suitable for simple forms with minimal validation requirements.

```
<template>
  <div>
    <form @submit.prevent="submitForm">
      <div>
        <label for="username">Username:</label>
        <input type="text" id="username" v-model="username" />
        <span v-if="usernameError">{{ usernameError }}</span>
      </div>
      <div>
        <label for="email">Email:</label>
        <input type="email" id="email" v-model="email" />
        <span v-if="emailError">{{ emailError }}</span>
      </div>
      <button type="submit">Submit</button>
    </form>
  </div>
</template>

<script>
export default {
  data() {
    return {
      username: '',
      email: '',
    };
  },
  computed: {
    usernameError() {
      if (this.username.length < 3) {
        return 'Username must be at least 3 characters long.';
      }
      return '';
    },
    emailError() {
      const emailPattern = /^[^\s@]+@[^\s@]+\.[^\s@]+$/;
      if (!this.email.match(emailPattern)) {
        return 'Please enter a valid email address.';
      }
      return '';
    },
  },
  methods: {
    submitForm() {
      if (!this.usernameError && !this.emailError) {
```

```
      // Form submission logic
      alert('Form submitted successfully!');
    }
   },
  },
 }
</script>
```

Validation with Vue Custom Directives

Custom directives can be used to encapsulate validation logic and apply it directly to form elements. This approach makes the validation logic reusable and more maintainable.

```
<template>
  <div>
    <form @submit.prevent="submitForm">
      <div>
        <label for="username">Username:</label>
        <input
          type="text"
          id="username"
          v-model="username"
          v-validate:username="{ minLength: 3 }"
        />
        <span>{{ validationErrors.username }}</span>
      </div>
      <div>
        <label for="email">Email:</label>
        <input
          type="email"
          id="email"
          v-model="email"
          v-validate:email="{ pattern: /^[^\s@]+@[^\s@]+\.[^\s@]+$/ }"
        />
        <span>{{ validationErrors.email }}</span>
      </div>
      <button type="submit">Submit</button>
    </form>
  </div>
</template>

<script>
Vue.directive('validate', {
  bind(el, binding, vnode) {
    const validationRules = binding.value;
    el.addEventListener('blur', () => {
      const field = binding.arg;
      const value = el.value;
      let error = '';

      if (validationRules.minLength && value.length < validationRules.minLength) {
        error = `Must be at least ${validationRules.minLength} characters.`;
      } else if (validationRules.pattern && !value.match(validationRules.pattern)) {
        error = 'Invalid format.';
      }
```

```
            vnode.context.$set(vnode.context.validationErrors, fi
eld, error);
        });
    },
});

export default {
  data() {
    return {
      username: '',
      email: '',
      validationErrors: {
        username: '',
        email: '',
      },
    };
  },
  methods: {
    submitForm() {
      if (!this.validationErrors.username && !this.validati
onErrors.email) {
        // Form submission logic
        alert('Form submitted successfully!');
      }
    },
  },
}
</script>
```

Using Vue Form Libraries

For more complex form validations, utilizing a form validation library like `Vuelidate` or `VeeValidate` can be extremely beneficial. These libraries provide comprehensive validation functionalities and integrate seamlessly with Vue.

Vuelidate

Below is an example of how to use Vuelidate for form validation.

```vue
<template>
  <div>
    <form @submit.prevent="submitForm">
      <div>
        <label for="username">Username:</label>
        <input
          type="text"
          id="username"
          v-model="username"
          :class="{ 'is-invalid': $v.username.$error }"
        />
        <span v-if="!$v.username.required">Username is required.</span>
        <span v-if="!$v.username.minLength">Minimum length is 3 characters.</span>
      </div>
      <div>
        <label for="email">Email:</label>
        <input
          type="email"
          id="email"
          v-model="email"
          :class="{ 'is-invalid': $v.email.$error }"
        />
        <span v-if="!$v.email.required">Email is required.</span>
        <span v-if="!$v.email.email">Must be a valid email.</span>
      </div>
      <button type="submit">Submit</button>
    </form>
  </div>
</template>

<script>
import { required, minLength, email } from 'vuelidate/lib/validators';
import { validationMixin } from 'vuelidate';

export default {
  mixins: [validationMixin],
  data() {
    return {
      username: '',
      email: '',
    };
  },
```

```
    validations: {
      username: {
        required,
        minLength: minLength(3),
      },
      email: {
        required,
        email,
      },
    },
    methods: {
      submitForm() {
        this.$v.$touch();
        if (!this.$v.$invalid) {
          // Form submission logic
          alert('Form submitted successfully!');
        }
      },
    },
  }
</script>
```

VeeValidate

Below is an example of how to use VeeValidate for form validation.

```html
<template>
  <div>
    <ValidationObserver v-slot="{ handleSubmit }">
      <form @submit.prevent="handleSubmit(submitForm)">
        <div>
          <label for="username">Username:</label>
          <ValidationProvider name="Username" rules="required|min:3" v-slot="{ errors }">
            <input type="text" id="username" v-model="username" />
            <span>{{ errors[0] }}</span>
          </ValidationProvider>
        </div>
        <div>
          <label for="email">Email:</label>
          <ValidationProvider name="Email" rules="required|email" v-slot="{ errors }">
            <input type="email" id="email" v-model="email" />
            <span>{{ errors[0] }}</span>
          </ValidationProvider>
        </div>
        <button type="submit">Submit</button>
      </form>
    </ValidationObserver>
  </div>
</template>

<script>
import { ValidationObserver, ValidationProvider } from 'vee-validate';
import { required, min, email } from 'vee-validate/dist/rules';
import { extend } from 'vee-validate';

extend('required', required);
extend('min', min);
extend('email', email);

export default {
  components: {
    ValidationObserver,
    ValidationProvider,
  },
  data() {
    return {
      username: '',
```

```
      email: '',
    };
  },
  methods: {
    submitForm() {
      // Form submission logic
      alert('Form submitted successfully!');
    },
  },
}
</script>
```

Conclusion

Form validation is a multifaceted task that can be tackled in several ways in Vue.js. From basic methods using computed properties to more complex solutions with custom directives or external libraries like Vuelidate and VeeValidate, Vue.js offers versatile options to ensure the integrity of user-submitted data. Select the method that best fits the complexity and requirements of your application.

7.4. Handling Form Submissions

Handling form submissions in Vue.js involves two primary steps: capturing the submitted data and performing an appropriate action, such as sending the data to a server or updating the app's state. This process leverages Vue's reactivity system and event handling capabilities to make dynamic and interactive web forms.

Basic Form Submission

In Vue, you can listen for form submissions using the `@submit` event handler. This approach allows you to call a JavaScript function when the form is submitted. Here's a basic example to illustrate this:

```vue
<template>
  <form @submit.prevent="handleSubmit">
    <label for="name">Name:</label>
    <input type="text" v-model="name" id="name" />

    <label for="email">Email:</label>
    <input type="email" v-model="email" id="email" />

    <button type="submit">Submit</button>
    <p>Submitted: {{ submittedData }}</p>
  </form>
</template>

<script>
export default {
  data() {
    return {
      name: '',
      email: '',
      submittedData: null
    };
  },
  methods: {
    handleSubmit() {
      this.submittedData = {
        name: this.name,
        email: this.email
      };
      console.log('Form data:', this.submittedData);
      // Perform further actions such as sending data to a server
    }
  }
};
</script>
```

The `@submit.prevent` directive prevents the default browser behavior of reloading the page when the form is submitted. The `handleSubmit` method captures and processes the form data.

Sending Data to a Server

For a more practical example, you might need to send the form data to a server. This typically involves making an HTTP request using libraries like Axios. Here's how you can accomplish this:

First, install Axios if you haven't already:

```
npm install axios
```

Next, modify the previous form submission example to include an HTTP POST request:

```vue
<template>
  <form @submit.prevent="handleSubmit">
    <label for="name">Name:</label>
    <input type="text" v-model="name" id="name" />

    <label for="email">Email:</label>
    <input type="email" v-model="email" id="email" />

    <button type="submit">Submit</button>
    <p v-if="responseMessage">{{ responseMessage }}</p>
  </form>
</template>

<script>
import axios from 'axios';

export default {
  data() {
    return {
      name: '',
      email: '',
      responseMessage: ''
    };
  },
  methods: {
    async handleSubmit() {
      const formData = {
        name: this.name,
        email: this.email
      };

      try {
        const response = await axios.post('https://example.com/api/form', formData);
        this.responseMessage = 'Form submitted successfully!';
        console.log('Server response:', response.data);
      } catch (error) {
        this.responseMessage = 'Failed to submit form!';
        console.error('Submission error:', error);
      }
    }
  }
};
</script>
```

In this enhanced example, the `handleSubmit` method sends the form data to an example server endpoint (https://example.com/api/form) using Axios. The response from the server is handled to provide feedback to the user.

Handling Form Submission Errors

While working with form submissions, handling potential errors is crucial for providing a good user experience. This might involve validating server responses and informing the user about any issues that arise. You can use the `try...catch` block to handle such errors:

```
<template>
  <form @submit.prevent="handleSubmit">
    <label for="name">Name:</label>
    <input type="text" v-model="name" id="name" />

    <label for="email">Email:</label>
    <input type="email" v-model="email" id="email" />

    <button type="submit">Submit</button>
    <p v-if="responseMessage">{{ responseMessage }}</p>
  </form>
</template>

<script>
import axios from 'axios';

export default {
  data() {
    return {
      name: '',
      email: '',
      responseMessage: ''
    };
  },
  methods: {
    async handleSubmit() {
      const formData = {
        name: this.name,
        email: this.email
      };

      try {
        const response = await axios.post('https://example.com/api/form', formData);
        if (response.data.success) {
          this.responseMessage = 'Form submitted successfully!';
        } else {
          this.responseMessage = response.data.message;
        }
      } catch (error) {
        this.responseMessage = 'Failed to submit form. Please try again later.';
        console.error('Submission error:', error);
      }
    }
  }
}
```

```
};
</script>
```

Summary

Handling form submissions in Vue.js is a straightforward process that involves capturing form data, preventing default behaviors, and optionally sending the data to a server. By leveraging Vue's powerful reactivity system and event handling, you can create dynamic and interactive forms that provide a seamless user experience. Whether you're storing data locally or interacting with external APIs, the flexibility of Vue.js makes it a suitable choice for handling form submissions effectively.

8. Integrating Vue with Laravel and Other Backend Frameworks

8.1 Setting Up a Laravel Backend for Vue Integration

Integrating Vue.js with a Laravel backend is a powerful way to create dynamic and robust web applications. Laravel provides a comprehensive set of tools and an elegant syntax that allow you to easily set up a backend, while Vue.js offers a reactive and component-based structure for building rich user interfaces. In this section, we'll walk through setting up a Laravel backend to be used with Vue.js.

Prerequisites

Before diving into the setup, ensure you have the following installed on your development machine:

- PHP (>=7.3)
- Composer
- Node.js and npm
- Laravel Installer (optional but recommended)

Creating a New Laravel Project

First, you need to create a new Laravel project. Open your terminal and run the following command:

```
composer create-project --prefer-dist laravel/laravel vue-laravel-app
```

Navigate to the newly created project directory:

```
cd vue-laravel-app
```

Configuring Database Connection

Laravel uses environment variables to configure various settings, including database connections. Open the `.env` file in the root directory of your project and update the database settings accordingly. For example:

```
DB_CONNECTION=mysql
DB_HOST=127.0.0.1
DB_PORT=3306
DB_DATABASE=vue_laravel_db
DB_USERNAME=root
DB_PASSWORD=secret
```

After updating the `.env` file, run the database migrations to set up the database tables:

```
php artisan migrate
```

Setting Up Vue in Laravel

Laravel comes with built-in support for integrating Vue.js through Laravel Mix. Laravel Mix provides a clean, fluent API for defining Webpack build steps. To start using Vue within your Laravel project, you need to install the necessary npm dependencies.

First, ensure you are in the root directory of your project and install the required packages:

```
npm install
npm install vue vue-router
```

Next, open the `webpack.mix.js` file and make sure it includes Vue support:

```
const mix = require('laravel-mix');

mix.js('resources/js/app.js', 'public/js')
    .vue()
    .sass('resources/sass/app.scss', 'public/css');
```

Setting Up Vue Components

Go to the `resources/js` directory and open the `app.js` file. Replace its contents with the following:

```
import { createApp } from 'vue';
import App from './components/App.vue';

createApp(App).mount('#app');
```

Next, create a new Vue component. In the `resources/js/components` directory, create a file named `App.vue` with the following content:

```
<template>
    <div id="app">
        <h1>Welcome to Vue with Laravel!</h1>
    </div>
</template>

<script>
export default {
    name: 'App'
};
</script>

<style scoped>
h1 {
    color: #42b983;
}
</style>
```

Updating Blade Template

To render your Vue component, you need to update the main Blade template. Open the `resources/views/welcome.blade.php` file and replace its contents with the following:

```
<!DOCTYPE html>
<html lang="{{ str_replace('_', '-', app()->getLocale()) }}">
<head>
    <meta charset="utf-8">
    <meta name="viewport" content="width=device-width, initial-scale=1">
    <title>Laravel Vue Integration</title>
    <link href="{{ mix('css/app.css') }}" rel="stylesheet">
</head>
<body>
    <div id="app"></div>
    <script src="{{ mix('js/app.js') }}"></script>
</body>
</html>
```

Running the Application

After setting everything up, you can compile your assets and run the development server. Run the following commands in the terminal:

```
npm run dev
php artisan serve
```

Open your browser and navigate to `http://127.0.0.1:8000`. You should see the message "Welcome to Vue with Laravel!" indicating that Vue.js has been successfully integrated with your Laravel backend.

Conclusion

By following these steps, you have set up a basic Laravel backend and integrated it with Vue.js. This establishes the foundation for building a dynamic, full-stack web application using these powerful tools. In the subsequent sections, we will delve deeper into utilizing Laravel APIs with Vue components and explore more advanced integrations.

8.2 Using Laravel APIs with Vue Components

As we delve deeper into integrating Vue with Laravel, one of the essential aspects is utilizing Laravel APIs with Vue components. By leveraging Laravel's powerful API capabilities and Vue's reactive front-end, you can create highly dynamic and robust web applications. This subchapter will guide you through creating Laravel APIs and consuming them in Vue components with practical examples.

Setting Up a RESTful API in Laravel

Before we can use the API in our Vue components, we need to set up a RESTful API in Laravel. For this example, let's create a simple API to manage a list of tasks.

1. **Creating a Task Model and Migration:**

Run the following Artisan command to create a Task model and migration:

```
php artisan make:model Task -m
```

This command will generate a `Task` model and a migration file. Open the migration file located in `database/migrations` and add the columns for the task:

```php
public function up()
{
    Schema::create('tasks', function (Blueprint $table) {
        $table->id();
        $table->string('title');
        $table->text('description')->nullable();
        $table->boolean('completed')->default(false);
        $table->timestamps();
    });
}
```

Run the migration to create the `tasks` table:

```
php artisan migrate
```

2. **Creating a Task Controller:**

Generate a controller to handle CRUD operations for tasks:

```
php artisan make:controller TaskController --resource
```

Implement basic API methods in the `TaskController`:

```php
use App\Models\Task;
use Illuminate\Http\Request;

class TaskController extends Controller
{
    public function index()
    {
        return Task::all();
    }

    public function store(Request $request)
    {
        $task = Task::create($request->all());
        return response()->json($task, 201);
    }

    public function show($id)
    {
        return Task::find($id);
    }

    public function update(Request $request, $id)
    {
        $task = Task::findOrFail($id);
        $task->update($request->all());
        return response()->json($task, 200);
    }

    public function destroy($id)
    {
        Task::destroy($id);
        return response()->json(null, 204);
    }
}
```

3. **Defining API Routes:**

Open the `routes/api.php` file and define routes for the Task API:

```php
Route::apiResource('tasks', TaskController::class);
```

Fetching API Data in Vue Components

From the front-end, you can use axios for making HTTP requests to the Laravel API. First, install axios if you haven't already:

```
npm install axios
```

Displaying Tasks in a Vue Component
   1. **Creating the TaskList Component:**

Create a new Vue component called `TaskList.vue`:

```vue
<template>
  <div>
    <h1>Tasks</h1>
    <ul>
      <li v-for="task in tasks" :key="task.id">
        {{ task.title }} - {{ task.completed ? "Completed" : "Pending" }}
      </li>
    </ul>
  </div>
</template>

<script>
import axios from 'axios';

export default {
  data() {
    return {
      tasks: []
    };
  },
  created() {
    this.fetchTasks();
  },
  methods: {
    fetchTasks() {
      axios.get('http://your-domain.com/api/tasks')
        .then(response => {
          this.tasks = response.data;
        })
        .catch(error => {
          console.error('There was an error fetching tasks: ', error);
        });
    }
  }
};
</script>

<style scoped>
/* Add your styles here */
</style>
```

2. **Registering the Component:**

Assuming you are using a Vue single-file component structure in resources/js and have an App.vue file, register the newly created TaskList component:

```
<template>
  <div id="app">
    <task-list></task-list>
  </div>
</template>

<script>
import TaskList from './components/TaskList.vue';

export default {
  components: {
    TaskList
  }
};
</script>

<style>
/* Add your styles here */
</style>
```

Creating New Tasks in Vue Components

Let's add a form to create new tasks from the TaskList component.

1. **Updating TaskList Component to Include a Form:**

```vue
<template>
  <div>
    <h1>Tasks</h1>
    <ul>
      <li v-for="task in tasks" :key="task.id">
        {{ task.title }} - {{ task.completed ? "Completed" : "Pending" }}
      </li>
    </ul>
    <form @submit.prevent="createTask">
      <input v-model="newTask.title" placeholder="Task title" required>
      <textarea v-model="newTask.description" placeholder="Task description"></textarea>
      <button type="submit">Add Task</button>
    </form>
  </div>
</template>

<script>
import axios from 'axios';

export default {
  data() {
    return {
      tasks: [],
      newTask: {
        title: '',
        description: '',
        completed: false
      }
    };
  },
  created() {
    this.fetchTasks();
  },
  methods: {
    fetchTasks() {
      axios.get('http://your-domain.com/api/tasks')
        .then(response => {
          this.tasks = response.data;
        })
        .catch(error => {
          console.error('There was an error fetching tasks: ', error);
        });
    },
```

```
    createTask() {
      axios.post('http://your-domain.com/api/tasks', this.n
ewTask)
        .then(response => {
          this.tasks.push(response.data);
          this.newTask.title = '';
          this.newTask.description = '';
        })
        .catch(error => {
          console.error('There was an error creating the ta
sk:', error);
        });
    }
  }
};
</script>

<style scoped>
/* Add your styles here */
</style>
```

This example demonstrates how to create a simple task management system using Laravel APIs and Vue components. By following these steps, you can apply similar techniques to develop more complex applications and fully leverage the potential of combining Laravel's backend capabilities with Vue's frontend flexibility.

8.3 Integrating Vue with Other Backend Frameworks

In modern web development, it's common to integrate Vue.js with various backend frameworks to build interactive and dynamic applications. This subchapter will explore how to integrate Vue with some popular backends such as Node.js with Express, Django, and Ruby on Rails. We will cover setting up the backend server, creating RESTful APIs, and integrating those APIs with Vue components.

Setting Up an Express Backend for Vue Integration

Express is a minimal and flexible Node.js web application framework that provides a robust set of features to build web and mobile applications. To get started, first, set up an Express server.

Step-by-Step Guide

1. **Initialize a new Node.js project**:

    Open your terminal and run:

    ```
    mkdir vue-express-backend
    cd vue-express-backend
    npm init -y
    ```

2. **Install dependencies**:

    ```
    npm install express body-parser cors
    ```

3. **Create an Express server**:

    Create a file named `server.js`:

    ```
    const express = require('express');
    const bodyParser = require('body-parser');
    const cors = require('cors');
    ```

```
const app = express();
const PORT = 3000;

app.use(cors());
app.use(bodyParser.json());

// Dummy endpoint
app.get('/api/greeting', (req, res) => {
  res.json({ message: 'Hello from Express!' });
});

app.listen(PORT, () => {
  console.log(`Server is running on http://localhost:${PORT}`);
});
```

Integrating Vue with an Express Backend

With the backend set up, we can now integrate it with a Vue frontend.

Step-by-Step Guide

1. **Set up a new Vue project**:

   Use Vue CLI to create a new project:

   ```
   vue create vue-express-frontend
   cd vue-express-frontend
   npm install axios
   ```

2. **Fetch data from Express API in a Vue component**:

   Edit `src/components/HelloWorld.vue` to fetch and display data from the Express API:

   ```
   <template>
     <div class="hello">
       <h1>{{ message }}</h1>
     </div>
   </template>

   <script>
   ```

```
import axios from 'axios';

export default {
  data() {
    return {
      message: ''
    };
  },
  created() {
    axios.get('http://localhost:3000/api/greeting')
      .then(response => {
        this.message = response.data.message;
      })
      .catch(error => {
        console.log(error);
      });
  }
};
</script>
```

Integrating Vue with a Django Backend

Django is a high-level Python web framework that encourages rapid development and clean, pragmatic design. Let's dive into setting up a Django backend and integrating it with Vue.

Step-by-Step Guide

1. **Set up a new Django project:**

   ```
   django-admin startproject vue_django_backend
   cd vue_django_backend
   python manage.py startapp api
   ```

2. **Configure Django to serve a REST API:**

   Install Django REST framework and CORS headers:

   ```
   pip install djangorestframework django-cors-headers
   ```

   Add them to `INSTALLED_APPS` in `settings.py`:

   ```
   INSTALLED_APPS = [
       ...
   ```

```
    'rest_framework',
    'corsheaders',
]

MIDDLEWARE = [
    ...
    'corsheaders.middleware.CorsMiddleware',
]

CORS_ORIGIN_ALLOW_ALL = True
```

Create a simple API endpoint in `api/views.py`:

```
from rest_framework.views import APIView
from rest_framework.response import Response

class GreetingView(APIView):
    def get(self, request):
        return Response({"message": "Hello from Django!"})
```

Add the URL configuration in `api/urls.py`:

```
from django.urls import path
from .views import GreetingView

urlpatterns = [
    path('greeting/', GreetingView.as_view(), name='greeting'),
]
```

Include `api/urls.py` in the main `urls.py`:

```
from django.contrib import admin
from django.urls import path, include

urlpatterns = [
    path('admin/', admin.site.urls),
    path('api/', include('api.urls')),
]
```

3. **Fetch data from Django API in Vue**:

    Create a new Vue project or use an existing one and update a component to fetch data:

```
axios.get('http://localhost:8000/api/greeting/')
  .then(response => {
    this.message = response.data.message;
  })
  .catch(error => {
    console.log(error);
  });
```

Integrating Vue with a Ruby on Rails Backend

Ruby on Rails is a server-side web application framework written in Ruby under the MIT License. Rails is a model-view-controller (MVC) framework, providing default structures for a database, a web service, and web pages.

Step-by-Step Guide

1. **Set up a new Rails project**:

   ```
   rails new vue_rails_backend --api
   cd vue_rails_backend
   ```

2. **Create a Rails controller for the API**:

   ```
   rails generate controller Api::V1::Greetings index
   ```

   Define the index action in `app/controllers/api/v1/greetings_controller.rb`:

   ```
   module Api
     module V1
       class GreetingsController < ApplicationController
         def index
           render json: { message: 'Hello from Rails!' }
         end
       end
     end
   end
   ```

   Add the route in `config/routes.rb`:

```
namespace :api do
  namespace :v1 do
    resources :greetings, only: [:index]
  end
end
```

3. **Fetch data from Rails API in Vue**:

    After setting up the Rails server, fetch data in the Vue component:

    ```
    axios.get('http://localhost:3000/api/v1/greetings')
        .then(response => {
          this.message = response.data.message;
        })
        .catch(error => {
          console.log(error);
        });
    ```

Conclusion

Integrating Vue.js with backend frameworks like Express, Django, and Ruby on Rails allows you to harness the power of Vue's reactive capabilities while leveraging robust server-side operations. By following the steps outlined above, you can easily set up your backend server, create RESTful APIs, and connect them to your Vue components to build dynamic and full-fledged applications.

8.4 Common Issues and Solutions in Integrating Vue with Backends

When integrating Vue.js with Laravel and other backend frameworks, developers often encounter common issues that can interrupt smooth workflow and application performance. Here, we will explore these common issues and their corresponding solutions, focusing on both Laravel backends and other popular backend frameworks. By leveraging these solutions, you can enhance the integration process and ensure a robust and maintainable application.

Cross-Origin Resource Sharing (CORS) Issues

Issue: When your Vue application is hosted on a different domain than your backend, you might encounter CORS issues, which prevents the Vue application from accessing the backend resources.

Solution: Ensure that your backend server is configured to allow cross-origin requests. In Laravel, you can configure CORS in the `app/Http/Middleware/` directory.

Laravel Example:

```php
// app/Http/Middleware/Cors.php
namespace App\Http\Middleware;

use Closure;

class Cors
{
    public function handle($request, Closure $next)
    {
        return $next($request)
            ->header('Access-Control-Allow-Origin', '*')
            ->header('Access-Control-Allow-Methods', 'GET, POST, PUT, DELETE, OPTIONS')
            ->header('Access-Control-Allow-Headers', 'Content-Type, Authorization');
    }
}
```

Then, register the middleware in app/Http/Kernel.php.

```php
// app/Http/Kernel.php
protected $middleware = [
    // ...
    \App\Http\Middleware\Cors::class,
];
```

This will configure your Laravel application to handle CORS, permitting requests from any origin.

CSRF Token Mismatch

Issue: When making authenticated requests, Vue.js may encounter a "CSRF token mismatch" issue because the token isn't included correctly.

Solution: Retrieve the CSRF token from the HTML meta tag and send it with your Axios or Fetch API requests.

Vue Axios Example:

```js
// resources/js/app.js
import axios from 'axios';

axios.defaults.headers.common['X-CSRF-TOKEN'] = document.querySelector('meta[name="csrf-token"]').getAttribute('content');
```

Make sure you have the CSRF meta tag in your HTML header:

```html
<!-- resources/views/layouts/app.blade.php -->
<meta name="csrf-token" content="{{ csrf_token() }}">
```

Authentication Handling

Issue: Handling authentication and maintaining sessions across your Vue frontend and backend can be challenging.

Solution: Utilize Laravel's built-in authentication services and integrate them seamlessly with Vue. Use Laravel Passport or Sanctum for API authentication.

Laravel Sanctum Example:

1. Install Sanctum:

```
composer require laravel/sanctum
```

2. Publish Sanctum configuration:

```
php artisan vendor:publish --provider="Laravel\Sanctum\SanctumServiceProvider"
```

3. Configure Sanctum middleware:

```php
// app/Http/Kernel.php
protected $middlewareGroups = [
    'web' => [
        // ...
        \Laravel\Sanctum\Http\Middleware\EnsureFrontendRequestsAreStateful::class,
        // ...
    ],
];
```

4. Use Sanctum in your Vue frontend:

```js
// resources/js/app.js
import axios from 'axios';

axios.defaults.withCredentials = true;

// Login component
axios.post('http://your-laravel-app.test/login', {
    email: this.email,
    password: this.password
}).then(response => {
    console.log('Logged in successfully');
}).catch(error => {
    console.error('Login failed', error);
});
```

API Versioning

Issue: Difficulty in managing different versions of the API, leading to breaking changes that affect the frontend.

Solution: Implement API versioning on your backend to ensure backward compatibility. This can be done by creating versioned routes in Laravel.

Laravel Versioning Example:

```php
// routes/api.php

Route::prefix('v1')->group(function () {
    Route::get('users', 'Api\v1\UserController@index');
    Route::post('login', 'Api\v1\AuthController@login');
});

Route::prefix('v2')->group(function () {
    Route::get('users', 'Api\v2\UserController@index');
    Route::post('login', 'Api\v2\AuthController@login');
});
```

Backend Environment Configuration

Issue: Managing different environment configurations for development, staging, and production can be complex.

Solution: Utilize environment variables for configuration settings. In Laravel, you can achieve this with the .env file:

```
# .env
APP_URL=http://localhost
API_URL=http://api.localhost
```

Access these variables in your Vue application by creating a configuration file that reads these values:

Vue Axios Configuration:

```
// resources/js/axios-config.js
import axios from 'axios';

axios.defaults.baseURL = process.env.MIX_API_URL;

export default axios;
```

By applying these solutions, you can address common issues in integrating Vue.js with backend frameworks, thereby facilitating a smoother development experience and more robust applications.

9. Testing and Debugging Vue Applications

9.1 Understanding the Basics of Testing in Vue.js

Testing is a critical aspect of modern web development, ensuring the reliability, quality, and maintainability of applications. Vue.js, like other contemporary frameworks, offers robust tools and practices for testing components, views, and the overall functionality of your application. This subchapter delves into the fundamental concepts and tools needed to start testing Vue.js applications effectively.

The Importance of Testing

In any development cycle, bugs and errors can emerge, causing breakdowns in functionality. Testing helps catch these issues early, making it easier to maintain and scale the application. Additionally, tests serve as documentation, providing clarity on how different parts of the application should behave.

Types of Tests in Vue.js

When testing Vue.js applications, different types of tests serve various purposes:

- **Unit Tests**: Focus on testing individual components in isolation to ensure that each part functions correctly.
- **Integration Tests**: Check the interaction between different components to ensure they work together seamlessly.
- **End-to-End (E2E) Tests**: Simulate user interactions with the application to test the entire flow from start to finish.

Testing Methods and Libraries

Vue.js leverages several libraries and tools to facilitate testing. Below are some of the most commonly used:

- **Jest**: A powerful testing framework designed to work with JavaScript, providing all the needed functionality out of the box.
- **Vue Test Utils**: A utility library specifically designed for testing Vue components.
- **Cypress**: An end-to-end testing framework that makes it easy to set up, write, and run tests.

Setting Up Testing Environment

To get started with testing in Vue.js, you need to set up the testing environment. Here's a basic setup using Jest and Vue Test Utils:

1. **Install Dependencies**: Ensure you have Vue CLI installed. If not, install it using npm or yarn:

    ```
    npm install -g @vue/cli
    ```

    Create a new Vue project if you don't have one:

    ```
    vue create my-vue-app
    ```

    Navigate to the project directory:

    ```
    cd my-vue-app
    ```

    Add Jest and Vue Test Utils:

    ```
    vue add unit-jest
    ```

2. **Folder Structure**: By default, Vue CLI creates a `tests/unit` directory. Here, you can place your unit tests.

Writing a Simple Unit Test

Let's write a unit test for a basic Vue component. Consider the following `HelloWorld.vue` component:

```
<template>
  <div>
    <p>{{ msg }}</p>
  </div>
</template>

<script>
export default {
  name: 'HelloWorld',
  props: {
    msg: {
      type: String,
      required: true
    }
  }
}
</script>
```

Here's a simple test to check if the component renders the message correctly:

```
import { shallowMount } from '@vue/test-utils';
import HelloWorld from '@/components/HelloWorld.vue';

describe('HelloWorld.vue', () => {
  it('renders props.msg when passed', () => {
    const msg = 'Hello World';
    const wrapper = shallowMount(HelloWorld, {
      propsData: { msg }
    });
    expect(wrapper.text()).toMatch(msg);
  });
});
```

In this test:

- We use `shallowMount` from `@vue/test-utils` to mount the `HelloWorld` component.

- We pass the `msg` prop to the component and check if the rendered text matches the prop value using Jest's `expect` function.

Running Tests

Run your tests using the Vue CLI with the following command:

```
npm run test:unit
```

You should see the test results in your terminal, indicating whether the tests passed or failed.

Conclusion

Understanding the basics of testing in Vue.js is the first step towards building robust and maintainable web applications. By employing unit tests, integration tests, and end-to-end tests, you ensure that your components and application functions are as expected. With tools like Jest, Vue Test Utils, and Cypress, you have a powerful toolkit at your disposal to facilitate thorough testing. In the following subchapters, we will explore these types of tests in greater detail and see more examples of how to implement them in your Vue.js applications.

9.2 Writing Unit Tests for Vue Components

In modern web development, ensuring the reliability of your application through automated testing is crucial. Unit tests allow you to test individual components in isolation, ensuring they function correctly under different conditions. In this subchapter, we will focus on writing unit tests for Vue components. We will cover the setup, structure, and best practices for creating effective unit tests using popular tools like Jest and Vue Test Utils.

Introduction to Unit Testing in Vue

To effectively write unit tests for Vue components, it's essential to first understand the concept of unit testing. Unit testing involves testing individual pieces of code, such as functions or components, in isolation to verify their correctness. This not only helps in catching bugs early in the development process but also ensures that each unit of your application behaves as expected.

Setting Up Your Testing Environment

Before we dive into writing tests, we need to set up our testing environment. The Vue CLI provides an easy way to add Jest and Vue Test Utils to your project.

1. **Install the necessary packages:**

   ```
   vue add unit-jest
   ```

   This command will install Jest and the Vue Test Utils library, set up the necessary configuration, and create some initial test files.

2. **Project Structure:**

Once the setup is complete, you will typically have a `tests` directory in your project root, specifically `tests/unit` for unit tests.

Writing Your First Unit Test

Let's start by writing a simple unit test for a Vue component. Assume we have a `HelloWorld.vue` component:

```
<template>
  <div>
    <h1>{{ msg }}</h1>
  </div>
</template>

<script>
export default {
  name: 'HelloWorld',
  props: {
    msg: String
  }
}
</script>
```

To test this component, create a new test file in the `tests/unit` directory called `HelloWorld.spec.js`:

```
import { shallowMount } from '@vue/test-utils';
import HelloWorld from '@/components/HelloWorld.vue';

describe('HelloWorld.vue', () => {
  it('renders props.msg when passed', () => {
    const msg = 'new message';
    const wrapper = shallowMount(HelloWorld, {
      propsData: { msg }
    });
    expect(wrapper.text()).toMatch(msg);
  });
});
```

In this test, we use `shallowMount` from Vue Test Utils to create a shallow-rendered component instance. This test verifies that the `msg` prop is rendered correctly.

Testing Component Methods

Next, let's add more complexity by testing a method in a Vue component. Consider the following `Counter.vue` component:

```
<template>
  <div>
    <button @click="increment">Increment</button>
    <p>{{ count }}</p>
  </div>
</template>

<script>
export default {
  name: 'Counter',
  data() {
    return {
      count: 0
    };
  },
  methods: {
    increment() {
      this.count += 1;
    }
  }
}
</script>
```

Create a test file called `Counter.spec.js`:

```
import { shallowMount } from '@vue/test-utils';
import Counter from '@/components/Counter.vue';

describe('Counter.vue', () => {
  it('increments count when button is clicked', async () => {
    const wrapper = shallowMount(Counter);
    await wrapper.find('button').trigger('click');
    expect(wrapper.vm.count).toBe(1);
  });
});
```

Here, we trigger a click event on the button and check if the `count` property has been incremented.

Testing Vuex in Components

Often, Vue components rely on Vuex for state management. Testing such components requires mocking the Vuex store. Let's consider a component `Profile.vue` that fetches user data from a Vuex store:

```
<template>
  <div>
    <p>{{ userName }}</p>
  </div>
</template>

<script>
export default {
  name: 'Profile',
  computed: {
    userName() {
      return this.$store.state.userName;
    }
  },
  created() {
    this.$store.dispatch('fetchUser');
  }
}
</script>
```

Create a test file `Profile.spec.js`:

```js
import { shallowMount, createLocalVue } from '@vue/test-uti
ls';
import Vuex from 'vuex';
import Profile from '@/components/Profile.vue';

const localVue = createLocalVue();
localVue.use(Vuex);

describe('Profile.vue', () => {
  let store;
  let state;
  let actions;

  beforeEach(() => {
    state = {
      userName: 'John Doe'
    };

    actions = {
      fetchUser: jest.fn()
    };

    store = new Vuex.Store({
      state,
      actions
    });
  });

  it('renders userName from the store', () => {
    const wrapper = shallowMount(Profile, { store, localVue });
    expect(wrapper.text()).toContain('John Doe');
  });

  it('dispatches "fetchUser" action on created', () => {
    shallowMount(Profile, { store, localVue });
    expect(actions.fetchUser).toHaveBeenCalled();
  });
});
```

In this test, we create a mock Vuex store with the necessary state and actions, ensuring that our component interacts correctly with Vuex.

Mocking External Services

Sometimes, components interact with external services or APIs. Mocking these services during testing is essential to isolate the component's behavior. Suppose you have a component Weather.vue that fetches weather data:

```
<template>
  <div>
    <p>{{ weather }}</p>
    <button @click="getWeather">Get Weather</button>
  </div>
</template>

<script>
import axios from 'axios';

export default {
  name: 'Weather',
  data() {
    return {
      weather: ''
    };
  },
  methods: {
    async getWeather() {
      const response = await axios.get('http://api.weather.com/current');
      this.weather = response.data.weather;
    }
  }
}
</script>
```

Create a test file Weather.spec.js:

```
import { shallowMount } from '@vue/test-utils';
import axios from 'axios';
import Weather from '@/components/Weather.vue';

jest.mock('axios');

describe('Weather.vue', () => {
  it('fetches weather data on button click', async () => {
    const weatherData = { weather: 'Sunny' };
    axios.get.mockResolvedValue({ data: weatherData });

    const wrapper = shallowMount(Weather);
    await wrapper.find('button').trigger('click');
    expect(wrapper.vm.weather).toBe(weatherData.weather);
  });
});
```

Here, we use Jest's `mock` function to mock the `axios` library, ensuring our component fetches the mocked data.

Best Practices for Unit Testing

- **Isolate Tests:** Ensure each test runs in isolation, without any dependencies on other tests.
- **Test Edge Cases:** Test various input scenarios, including edge cases, to ensure robustness.
- **Mock Dependencies:** Mock external services, Vuex store, and other dependencies to focus solely on the component's behavior.
- **Keep Tests Simple:** Write clear and concise tests to improve readability and maintainability.
- **Automate Tests:** Integrate your tests into a continuous integration pipeline to automatically run them on each code change.

By following these principles and the examples provided, you can effectively write unit tests for your Vue components, ensuring a more reliable and maintainable codebase.

9.3 Performing End-to-End Testing with Vue.js

End-to-end (E2E) testing is an essential part of ensuring that your Vue.js applications work as intended from the user's perspective. E2E tests simulate real user interactions with your application, testing the entire flow from the frontend to the backend. This subchapter will guide you through setting up and writing E2E tests for Vue.js applications using Cypress, a popular E2E testing framework.

Setting Up Cypress

To start performing E2E tests with Vue.js, you need to integrate Cypress into your project. Follow these steps to set up Cypress:

1. Install Cypress via npm:

```
npm install cypress --save-dev
```

2. Initialize Cypress to create the default folder structure. Run the following command:

```
npx cypress open
```

This will open the Cypress Test Runner and create a `cypress` folder in your project with default directories for fixtures, integration tests, plugins, and support files.

Writing Your First E2E Test

Let's write a simple E2E test to verify that your Vue application's homepage loads correctly. Create a new test file in the `cypress/integration` folder:

```
touch cypress/integration/homepage.spec.js
```

Open homepage.spec.js and add the following code:

```
describe('Homepage', () => {
  it('should load successfully', () => {
    cy.visit('http://localhost:8080') // Change to your local server URL
    cy.contains('Welcome to Your Vue.js App')
  })
})
```

This test does the following: - Visits the homepage of your application. - Checks if the homepage contains the text "Welcome to Your Vue.js App".

Interacting with Page Elements

E2E tests often require interaction with different elements on your page. Cypress provides a variety of commands to simulate user actions. Here's an example of how to test a user login form:

```
describe('Login Form', () => {
  it('should log in successfully with correct credentials', () => {
    cy.visit('http://localhost:8080/login')

    // Type into form fields
    cy.get('input[name=username]').type('testuser')
    cy.get('input[name=password]').type('password123')

    // Submit the form
    cy.get('form').submit()

    // Check for successful login message
    cy.contains('Login successful')
  })
})
```

Testing Navigation

Vue Router is a crucial part of many Vue.js applications. You should write tests to ensure that navigation works correctly. Here's an example:

```
describe('Navigation', () => {
  it('should navigate to About page', () => {
    cy.visit('http://localhost:8080')
    cy.get('nav a[href="/about"]').click()
    cy.url().should('include', '/about')
    cy.contains('This is an about page')
  })
})
```

Mocking API Requests

In some cases, you may want to mock API requests to test different states of your application without relying on the backend. Cypress allows you to intercept and mock network requests:

```
describe('API Requests', () => {
  it('should display user data', () => {
    cy.server()
    cy.route('GET', '/api/users', [{ id: 1, name: 'John Doe' }])

    cy.visit('http://localhost:8080/users')

    cy.contains('John Doe')
  })
})
```

Running Tests in Continuous Integration

For continuous integration (CI), it is important to run your Cypress tests as part of your build pipeline. Here's how you can do it:

1. Add a Cypress script to your `package.json`:

```
"scripts": {
  "test:e2e": "cypress run"
}
```

2. Ensure Cypress runs during your CI pipeline. For example, if you're using GitHub Actions, you can add a configuration file `.github/workflows/ci.yml`:

```
name: CI

on: [push, pull_request]

jobs:
  test:
    runs-on: ubuntu-latest

    steps:
    - uses: actions/checkout@v2
    - name: Use Node.js
      uses: actions/setup-node@v1
      with:
        node-version: '12'
    - run: npm install
    - run: npm run test:e2e
```

This configuration ensures that Cypress tests are executed automatically with every push or pull request.

Conclusion

End-to-end testing is a powerful technique for ensuring your Vue.js applications function correctly from the user's perspective. By setting up Cypress, you can write robust tests that interact with your application and verify that all parts of your stack are integrating smoothly. Integrating these tests into your CI pipeline helps maintain the quality and reliability of your application over time.

9.4 Debugging Common Issues in Vue Applications

Debugging is a crucial part of the development process. Despite your best efforts in writing flawless code and comprehensive tests, bugs will inevitably occur. In this section, we'll explore common issues you may encounter in Vue applications and strategies for resolving them.

Identifying Errors with Vue Devtools

The Vue Devtools extension is an indispensable resource for debugging Vue applications. You can use it to inspect the component hierarchy, view component data, and monitor the Vuex state, among other functionalities.

To install Vue Devtools, visit the following URLs: - Chrome: https://chrome.google.com/webstore/detail/vuejs-devtools/nhdogjmejiglipccpnnnanhbledajbpd - Firefox: https://addons.mozilla.org/en-US/firefox/addon/vue-js-devtools/

Once installed, you can access the Vue tab in your browser's developer tools. Here, you can inspect elements, view the component tree, and see the current state of each component.

```
<template>
  <div id="app">
    <MyComponent></MyComponent>
  </div>
</template>
```

With Vue Devtools, you can select `MyComponent` and see all its properties and data in real-time.

Console Logging

Console logging is one of the simplest and most effective debugging techniques. Adding `console.log` statements at various points in your code can help you trace the flow of data and identify where things might be going wrong.

```
methods: {
  fetchData() {
    console.log('Fetching data...');
    axios.get('/api/data')
      .then(response => {
        console.log('Data fetched:', response.data);
        this.data = response.data;
      })
      .catch(error => {
        console.error('Error fetching data:', error);
      });
  }
}
```

Handling Common Errors

Undefined or Null Data

One of the most frequent issues in Vue applications is attempting to use data that is `undefined` or `null`. This often results in errors like "Cannot read property 'X' of undefined."

To handle such cases, ensure that your data is initialized properly. You can use the `v-if` directive to conditionally render elements only when the data is available.

```
<template>
  <div v-if="data">
    <p>{{ data.message }}</p>
  </div>
  <div v-else>
    <p>Loading...</p>
  </div>
</template>

<script>
export default {
  data() {
    return {
      data: null
    };
  },
  created() {
    this.fetchData();
  },
  methods: {
    fetchData() {
      axios.get('/api/data')
        .then(response => {
          this.data = response.data;
        })
        .catch(error => {
          console.error('Error fetching data:', error);
        });
    }
  }
};
</script>
```

Incorrect Prop Types

Vue has a built-in mechanism for validating prop types. If you're passing the incorrect type of data to a component, it will throw a warning in development mode.

```
props: {
  count: {
    type: Number,
    required: true
  }
}
```

If you pass a string to the `count` prop, Vue will emit a warning in the console. Always validate your props to catch such errors early.

Reactive Data Issues

Sometimes, changes made to reactive data in Vue do not appear to update the DOM as expected. This generally happens due to limitations in Vue's reactivity system.

Adding New Properties to an Object

Vue cannot detect property addition or deletion on an object. To remedy this, use `Vue.set` for adding new properties.

```
this.$set(this.someObject, 'newProperty', 'newValue');
```

Array Mutations

Vue wraps array methods to ensure that they are reactive. However, direct array mutations like setting length or using the bracket notation may not trigger updates.

```
// Instead of
this.items[1] = 'new item';

// Use
this.$set(this.items, 1, 'new item');
```

Network Errors

Network requests can fail for various reasons, such as server errors or connectivity issues. Always handle promises returned by HTTP requests using `.catch` to log errors and update the UI accordingly.

```
axios.get('/api/items')
  .then(response => {
    this.items = response.data;
  })
  .catch(error => {
    console.error('Error fetching items:', error);
    this.errorMessage = 'Failed to load items.';
  });
```

By following these guidelines and leveraging the tools available, you can efficiently debug and resolve common issues in your Vue applications. Remember, debugging is an iterative process, involving careful inspection of code, understanding the root cause, and applying appropriate fixes.

10. Performance Optimization Techniques

10.1 Code Splitting

Code splitting is an essential performance optimization technique that involves breaking down your application's code into smaller, more manageable chunks. This allows for faster load times and improved performance, particularly for users on slower networks. In Vue.js, code splitting can be efficiently achieved through built-in features of Vue CLI and routing.

Benefits of Code Splitting

Before diving into the implementation, let's discuss the benefits of code splitting:

1. **Faster Initial Load Time**: By loading only the necessary code for the initial render, the initial page load time is significantly reduced.
2. **Improved Application Performance**: By loading parts of the application only when they are needed, you avoid bloating the user's browser with unused code.
3. **Better User Experience**: Users experience a smoother and faster application, as the perceived load time is reduced.

Basic Code Splitting with Vue Router

One of the most straightforward ways to implement code splitting in a Vue.js application is through route-based splitting with Vue Router. This can be achieved by using dynamic imports in your route configuration. Here's an example setup:

```javascript
// src/router/index.js

import Vue from 'vue';
import Router from 'vue-router';

Vue.use(Router);

const routes = [
  {
    path: '/',
    name: 'Home',
    component: () => import('../components/Home.vue')
  },
  {
    path: '/about',
    name: 'About',
    component: () => import('../components/About.vue')
  },
  {
    path: '/contact',
    name: 'Contact',
    component: () => import('../components/Contact.vue')
  }
];

export default new Router({
  mode: 'history',
  routes
});
```

In the above example, each route dynamically imports its corresponding component. This ensures that each component is loaded only when its route is visited, cutting down the initial load time for the application.

Code Splitting with Vue Components

Apart from routing, you can also employ code splitting at the component level. This is particularly useful when dealing with large components or third-party libraries that are not immediately needed.

Here's an example of achieving component-level code splitting:

```
// src/components/ParentComponent.vue

<template>
  <div>
    <button @click="LoadChildComponent">Load Child Component</button>
    <child-component v-if="isChildLoaded"></child-component>
  </div>
</template>

<script>
export default {
  data() {
    return {
      isChildLoaded: false
    };
  },
  methods: {
    async LoadChildComponent() {
      const { default: ChildComponent } = await import('./ChildComponent.vue');
      this.$options.components['child-component'] = ChildComponent;
      this.isChildLoaded = true;
    }
  }
};
</script>
```

In this example, ChildComponent is only imported and registered when the user clicks the button, thereby deferring the load until necessary.

Configuring Webpack for Advanced Code Splitting

Vue CLI uses Webpack for module bundling, and you can fine-tune Webpack configurations for advanced code splitting strategies. Vue CLI makes this seamless with its configuration files.

To customize Webpack's `splitChunks` configuration, you can modify `vue.config.js`:

```js
// vue.config.js
module.exports = {
  configureWebpack: {
    optimization: {
      splitChunks: {
        chunks: 'all',
        minSize: 20000,
        maxSize: 70000,
        cacheGroups: {
          defaultVendors: {
            test: /[\\/]node_modules[\\/]/,
            priority: -10
          },
          common: {
            name: 'common',
            minChunks: 2,
            priority: -5,
            reuseExistingChunk: true
          }
        }
      }
    }
  }
};
```

In this configuration, Webpack splits the application code into smaller chunks based on the defined rules. For instance, it ensures that imported dependencies from `node_modules` are separated into their own chunk and common modules used in multiple places are extracted into a separate `common` chunk.

Monitoring and Analyzing Performance

To measure the impact of code splitting, you can use tools like Webpack Bundle Analyzer. This can be integrated into your Vue CLI project quickly:

```
// vue.config.js
const BundleAnalyzerPlugin = require('webpack-bundle-analyz
er').BundleAnalyzerPlugin;

module.exports = {
  configureWebpack: {
    plugins: [
      new BundleAnalyzerPlugin()
    ]
  }
};
```

To run the bundle analyzer, update your `package.json` scripts:

```
{
  "scripts": {
    "analyze": "vue-cli-service build --report"
  }
}
```

Run the analyzer with:

```
npm run analyze
```

This opens a visualization of your bundle size and composition, helping you identify areas for further optimization.

Conclusion

Code splitting is a vital technique for optimizing the performance of Vue.js applications. By loading only the essential parts of your application at initial load and deferring the rest, you can greatly enhance your application's speed and responsiveness, significantly improving the user experience. With Vue CLI and Vue Router, you have powerful tools at your disposal to implement efficient code splitting.

10.2 Lazy Loading

Lazy loading is a performance optimization technique that allows you to defer the loading of resources until they are actually needed. In the context of Vue.js, lazy loading can be applied to various elements such as components, images, and external scripts. This strategy is particularly useful for improving the performance of applications by reducing the initial load time and delivering resources to the user on demand.

Benefits of Lazy Loading

1. **Improved Load Time:** By loading resources only when they are needed, you can significantly reduce the initial load time of your application.
2. **Reduced Bandwidth Consumption:** Since only the necessary resources are loaded, you save bandwidth, which is important for users on limited data plans.
3. **Better User Experience:** Faster load times contribute to a smoother user experience, keeping users engaged longer.

Lazy Loading Vue Components

In Vue.js, lazy loading of components is often achieved by leveraging dynamic imports. This way, the component is only loaded when it's actually needed.

Here's an example of how you can implement lazy loading for a Vue component:

```
// Define the route with a dynamic import
const routes = [
  {
    path: '/about',
    component: () => import(/* webpackChunkName: "about" */ './views/About.vue')
  }
]
```

In this example, the About.vue component will only be loaded when the /about route is visited.

Lazy Loading Images

Lazy loading images is another effective use of this technique. You can use third-party libraries like vue-lazyload to manage this easily.

1. **Installation:** First, install the library using npm.

```
npm install vue-lazyload
```

2. **Setup and Usage:** Then, set it up in your Vue application.

```
import Vue from 'vue'
import VueLazyload from 'vue-lazyload'

Vue.use(VueLazyload)

// Usage in your template
<img v-lazy="imageSrc" alt="Description">
```

The v-lazy directive ensures that the image is loaded only when it comes into the viewport.

Lazy Loading External Scripts

Sometimes, you may need to load external scripts like analytics or advertisement libraries. You can achieve this using a combination of dynamic imports and the `onload` event.

```
function loadExternalScript(url) {
  return new Promise((resolve, reject) => {
    const script = document.createElement('script')
    script.src = url
    script.onload = () => resolve()
    script.onerror = () => reject(new Error(`Script load error for ${url}`))
    document.head.appendChild(script)
  })
}

// Usage
loadExternalScript('https://example.com/external-script.js')
  .then(() => {
    // Script is loaded, you can now use it
  })
  .catch(error => {
    console.error(error)
  })
```

Best Practices for Lazy Loading

1. **Prioritize Critical Resources:** Always ensure that critical resources are not deferred, as this can negatively impact the user experience.
2. **Use Code Splitting:** Combine lazy loading with code splitting for even better performance.
3. **Fallback Mechanisms:** Implement fallback mechanisms to handle failed lazy loads gracefully.
4. **Monitor Performance:** Use tools like Google Lighthouse or WebPageTest to monitor the effectiveness of your lazy loading strategy.

Conclusion

By incorporating lazy loading into your Vue.js projects, you can create highly performant and user-friendly web applications. Whether it's components, images, or external scripts, deferring the load until necessary is a strategic way to optimize performance and enhance the user experience. In the next sections, we will dive deeper into other performance optimization techniques like memoization and optimizing dependencies to further enhance your Vue.js applications.

10.3 Memoization

Memoization is a powerful optimization technique used to improve the performance of your Vue.js applications by caching the results of expensive function calls and reusing the cached result when the same inputs occur again. In Vue.js, memoization can be particularly useful when dealing with expensive computations or repetitive renderings, enhancing both the speed and efficiency of your application.

Understanding Memoization

Memoization involves storing the results of a function call and returning the cached result when the same inputs are provided again. This technique reduces redundant computations, which can be especially beneficial when operations are resource-intensive or frequently invoked.

Here is a simple example to demonstrate the concept of memoization:

```
function memoize(fn) {
  const cache = new Map();
  return function(...args) {
    const key = JSON.stringify(args);
    if (cache.has(key)) {
      return cache.get(key);
    }
    const result = fn(...args);
    cache.set(key, result);
    return result;
  };
}
function expensiveFunction(num) {
  console.log('Computing...');
  return num * num;
}

const memoizedExpensiveFunction = memoize(expensiveFunction
);

console.log(memoizedExpensiveFunction(5));
console.log(memoizedExpensiveFunction(5));
```

In this example, the `expensiveFunction` is memoized, meaning it computes the result for the first call and caches it. On subsequent calls with the same argument, it retrieves the result from the cache, avoiding redundant computations.

Memoization in Vue.js

In a Vue.js application, memoization can be applied to computed properties, methods, or even entire components to avoid unnecessary recalculations.

Memoizing Computed Properties

Computed properties in Vue.js are inherently optimized to cache their results based on their dependencies. However, if you need more fine-grained control, you can explicitly memoize a computed property.

Below is an example of memoizing a computed property:

```
const expensiveComputation = memoize(function(number) {
  console.log('Computing...');
  return number * number;
});

new Vue({
  el: '#app',
  data() {
    return {
      number: 0,
    };
  },
  computed: {
    computedNumber() {
      return expensiveComputation(this.number);
    }
  },
  template: `<div>
              <input v-model="number" type="number">
              <p>Computed Number: {{ computedNumber }}</p>
            </div>`,
});
```

In the above example, the `expensiveComputation` function is memoized, ensuring that its computations are cached and reused whenever the same input is provided through the `number` data property.

Memoizing Methods

Apart from computed properties, you can also memoize methods. This can be particularly useful when methods perform complex data processing or heavy calculations.

```
new Vue({
  el: '#app',
  data() {
    return {
      number: 0,
    };
  },
  methods: {
    expensiveCalculation: memoize(function(number) {
      console.log('Calculating...');
      return number * number;
    })
  },
  template: `<div>
              <input v-model="number" type="number">
              <button @click="expensiveCalculation(number)">Compute</button>
              <p>Check console for cached results</p>
            </div>`,
});
```

Here, the expensiveCalculation method is memoized, enhancing the efficiency of repetitive calculations based on the same input values.

Real-World Application

Let's consider a real-world scenario where memoization can significantly enhance performance. Imagine a Vue.js application rendering a list of items with live search functionality. Each keystroke triggers a filter function to find the matching items, which could be expensive if the list is large.

Here is how you can memoize the search function:

```
const searchItems = memoize(function(items, query) {
  console.log('Filtering...');
  return items.filter(item => item.includes(query));
});

new Vue({
  el: '#app',
  data() {
    return {
      query: '',
      items: ['apple', 'banana', 'grape', 'orange', 'pineapple']
    };
  },
  computed: {
    filteredItems() {
      return searchItems(this.items, this.query);
    }
  },
  template: `<div>
            <input v-model="query" placeholder="Search items">
            <ul>
              <li v-for="item in filteredItems" :key="item">{{ item }}</li>
            </ul>
           </div>`,
});
```

In this example, the `searchItems` function is memoized to cache the filtered results for the same search query, ensuring that expensive list operations are minimized and the application performs efficiently even with large datasets.

Conclusion

Memoization is a crucial performance optimization technique that can significantly enhance the speed and efficiency of your Vue.js applications. By caching results of expensive computations and reusing them, you can minimize redundant operations and improve the overall user experience. Integrating memoization into your Vue.js components, methods, and computed properties is straightforward and can yield substantial performance gains.

10.4 Optimizing Dependencies

Dependencies are an integral part of any modern web application, including those built with Vue.js. Effective management and optimization of these dependencies can significantly enhance your application's performance. In this section, we will explore techniques to ensure your applications don't carry unnecessary baggage, leading to faster load times and improved user experiences.

Analyzing Bundle Size

One of the first steps in optimizing dependencies is to analyze your bundle size. This helps identify large or unnecessary modules that could be affecting your application's performance. Tools like Webpack Bundle Analyzer can be particularly useful.

```
# First, install Webpack Bundle Analyzer
npm install --save-dev webpack-bundle-analyzer

# Then add it to your Webpack configuration
const BundleAnalyzerPlugin = require('webpack-bundle-analyz
er').BundleAnalyzerPlugin;

module.exports = {
  //... other configurations
  plugins: [
    new BundleAnalyzerPlugin(),
  ],
};
```

Run your build process, and a interactive visual report of your bundle will be available, which can help you identify large or redundant dependencies:

```
npm run build
```

Visit `http://localhost:8888` to view the report.

Tree Shaking

Tree shaking is a feature of modern JavaScript bundlers like Webpack that remove dead code from your application. This technique is particularly effective when using ES6 modules. Make sure your libraries and modules support ES6 imports to fully benefit from tree shaking.

```
// Import only what you need
import { mapState } from 'vuex';

export default {
  computed: mapState({
    user: state => state.user,
  }),
};
```

By importing only the modules you need, you ensure that any unused code is not included in the final bundle.

Using CDN for External Libraries

Serving common libraries via a Content Delivery Network (CDN) can not only reduce the load on your server but can also benefit from caching across multiple sites. Libraries like Axios, Lodash, and Vue itself can be added via CDN.

```html
<!DOCTYPE html>
<html lang="en">
<head>
  <meta charset="UTF-8">
  <title>Vue App</title>
  <script src="https://cdn.jsdelivr.net/npm/vue@2.6.12"></script>
  <script src="https://cdn.jsdelivr.net/npm/axios@0.21.1"></script>
  <script src="https://cdn.jsdelivr.net/npm/lodash@4.17.21"></script>
</head>
<body>
  <div id="app">{{ message }}</div>
  <script>
    new Vue({
      el: '#app',
      data: {
        message: 'Hello, World!'
      }
    });
  </script>
</body>
</html>
```

Code Splitting Vendor Libraries

Vendor code typically refers to third-party libraries your application depends on. By splitting your vendor code from your application code, the browser can cache it independently, resulting in faster load times for repeat visitors.

In a Webpack configuration, you can specify the separation of vendor code:

```
module.exports = {
  //... other configurations
  optimization: {
    splitChunks: {
      cacheGroups: {
        vendor: {
          test: /[\\/]node_modules[\\/]/,
          name: 'vendors',
          chunks: 'all',
        },
      },
    },
  },
};
```

Removing Unused Dependencies

Over time, your project may accumulate dependencies that are no longer being used. Tools like depcheck can identify unused dependencies for removal.

```
# Install depcheck
npm install -g depcheck

# Run depcheck in your project directory
depcheck
```

Review the report and remove the unnecessary dependencies:

```
npm uninstall <package-name>
```

Optimizing Lodash Imports

Lodash is a powerful library, but it's also quite large. By importing Lodash functions individually, rather than the entire library, you can significantly reduce your bundle size.

```
// Instead of this
import _ from 'Lodash';

// Do this
import debounce from 'Lodash/debounce';

export default {
  methods: {
    handleResize: debounce(function () {
      console.log('Resized!');
    }, 500)
  }
};
```

Minimizing CSS Frameworks

Using comprehensive CSS frameworks can also contribute to larger bundle sizes. Consider using only the required parts of the framework or opt for lighter alternatives. For example, instead of including the entire Bulma CSS framework:

```
<Link href="https://cdnjs.cloudflare.com/ajax/libs/bulma/0.9.3/css/bulma.min.css" rel="stylesheet"/>
```

You could include only the necessary components or use a modular CSS framework like Tailwind CSS, which focuses on utility-first CSS.

Conclusion

Optimizing your dependencies is a continual process that requires regular maintenance and monitoring. By employing the strategies detailed in this section, you can significantly enhance the performance of your Vue.js applications, resulting in smoother user experiences and more efficient use of resources. Remember, the goal is not just reducing file sizes but improving overall application responsiveness.

Effective dependency optimization will allow your application to scale effortlessly while maintaining excellent performance characteristics.

11. Deploying Vue Applications

11.1. Preparing the Production Build

Deploying a Vue.js application involves more than just hosting your files on a server. To ensure that your application performs well in a production environment, you need to prepare a production build. This subchapter covers the steps and best practices for creating an optimized production build of your Vue.js application. We will utilize Vue CLI, which offers a set of default configurations optimized for production.

Using Vue CLI to Build for Production

Vue CLI makes it straightforward to create a production build. To begin, ensure that all your project dependencies are installed and up-to-date. You can do this by running:

```
npm install
```

Next, execute the build command:

```
npm run build
```

This command will generate optimized, minified files in a `dist` directory by default.

Understanding the Output Files

After running `npm run build`, you will see a new directory named `dist` in your project root. This directory contains your application's compiled and minified files. Typically, the directory structure will look something like this:

```
dist/
├── css/
│   └── app.<hash>.css
├── js/
│   └── app.<hash>.js
└── index.html
```

The `hash` in the filenames helps with cache busting, ensuring that users always get the latest version of your files.

Customizing the Build Configuration

Sometimes, you might need to customize the build configuration to meet specific needs, such as changing the output directory or tweaking the build process. Vue CLI allows this via the `vue.config.js` file.

For example, if you want to change the output directory from `dist` to `public`, you can modify `vue.config.js` as follows:

```
module.exports = {
  outputDir: 'public'
};
```

Environmental Variables

Using environment variables is crucial for configuring your application differently based on the environment (development, testing, production). Vue CLI uses `.env` files to define these variables.

For instance, you might have a `.env.production` file that contains:

```
VUE_APP_API_URL=https://api.production.com
```

In your Vue.js application, you can access this variable using `process.env.VUE_APP_API_URL`:

```
const apiUrl = process.env.VUE_APP_API_URL;
```

Tree Shaking and Code Splitting

Tree shaking and code splitting are techniques to optimize your application by reducing the final bundle size.

1. **Tree Shaking:** Vue CLI utilizes Webpack's tree shaking feature, which automatically removes unused code. There's usually no additional configuration required.

2. **Code Splitting:** You can define different chunks of your application to be loaded on demand. This is typically done using dynamic `import` in your Vue components:

```
const AsyncComponent = () => import(/* webpackChunkName: "async-component" */ './AsyncComponent.vue');
```

Linting and Formatting

Linting and formatting your code can catch potential errors and enforce code standards. Ensure that linting is part of your build process. You can add a script to your `package.json` to run ESLint:

```
{
  "scripts": {
    "lint": "eslint --ext .js,.vue src"
  }
}
```

Run the linting script before building your application:

```
npm run lint && npm run build
```

Testing Before Deployment

Before considering your build ready for deployment, ensure that all tests pass. Include a test script in your `package.json`:

```
{
  "scripts": {
    "test": "vue-cli-service test:unit"
  }
}
```

Run your tests:

```
npm run test
```

By following these steps, you will ensure that your Vue.js application is optimized and ready for deployment to a production environment. In the next subchapter, we'll delve into the necessary server configurations for hosting a Vue.js application effectively.

11.2. Server Configurations for Vue Apps

When deploying a Vue.js application, it is imperative to ensure the server configuration is tailored to guarantee optimal performance, security, and reliability. This subchapter delves into various server configurations suitable for Vue applications, examining static file servers, reverse proxies, and caching strategies, among others.

Basic Static File Server Setup

A Vue.js application, once built for production, consists mostly of static files. As such, a straightforward approach to serving these files is to use a static file server.

Using Nginx

Nginx is a popular web server that is well-suited for serving static files. Here is an example configuration to serve a Vue application using Nginx:

```
server {
    listen 80;
    server_name example.com;

    root /var/www/your-vue-app/dist;
    index index.html;

    location / {
        try_files $uri $uri/ /index.html;
    }

    location ~* \.(?:manifest|appcache|html?|xml|json)$ {
        add_header Cache-Control "no-store";
    }

    location ~* \.(?:css|js|woff2?|ico|png|svg|jpe?g|gif|map)$ {
        add_header Cache-Control "public, max-age=31536000, immutable";
    }
}
```

This configuration: 1. Listens on port 80 for HTTP requests. 2. Sets the root directory to your Vue app's `dist` folder. 3. Configures the `location /` block to handle routing, falling back to `index.html`. 4. Adds caching rules for different file types to optimize performance.

Reverse Proxy Server

In scenarios where the Vue.js application interacts frequently with an API, it's beneficial to employ a reverse proxy. This setup provides security benefits and simplifies the URL structure for clients.

Using Nginx

Here's how to configure Nginx to act as a reverse proxy for an API server and serve a Vue application simultaneously:

```
server {
    listen 80;
    server_name api.example.com;

    location /api/ {
        proxy_pass http://backend_api_server:3000/;
        proxy_set_header Host $host;
        proxy_set_header X-Real-IP $remote_addr;
        proxy_set_header X-Forwarded-For $proxy_add_x_forwarded_for;
        proxy_set_header X-Forwarded-Proto $scheme;
    }

    location / {
        root /var/www/your-vue-app/dist;
        try_files $uri $uri/ /index.html;
    }
}
```

This setup forwards all requests starting with `/api/` to an API server running on `http://backend_api_server:3000` while serving static files from the Vue app.

SSL/TLS Configuration

Securing your application with HTTPS is critical. Here's how you can configure Nginx to use SSL:

```
server {
    listen 80;
    server_name example.com;
    return 301 https://$host$request_uri;
}

server {
    listen 443 ssl;
    server_name example.com;

    ssl_certificate /etc/nginx/ssl/cert.pem;
    ssl_certificate_key /etc/nginx/ssl/cert.key;

    # SSL configuration
    ssl_protocols TLSv1.2 TLSv1.3;
    ssl_ciphers HIGH:!aNULL:!MD5;

    root /var/www/your-vue-app/dist;
    index index.html;

    location / {
        try_files $uri $uri/ /index.html;
    }
}
```

In this example: 1. All HTTP traffic is redirected to HTTPS. 2. The server listens on port 443 with SSL enabled. 3. SSL certificates and protocols are configured.

Caching Strategies

Effective caching can significantly improve the performance of your Vue app. Here are some strategies:

Browser Caching

Modify your server configuration to instruct browsers on how to cache resources:

```
location ~* \.(?:css|js|woff2?|ico|png|svg|jpe?g|gif|map)$
{
    add_header Cache-Control "public, max-age=31536000, immutable";
}
```

This tells the browser to cache static assets for one year.

Server-Side Caching

Implement server-side caching to reduce the load on your API server. Here's a simple configuration using Nginx's `proxy_cache`:

```
proxy_cache_path /data/nginx/cache levels=1:2 keys_zone=my_cache:10m max_size=1g inactive=60m use_temp_path=off;

server {
    listen 80;
    server_name api.example.com;

    location /api/ {
        proxy_cache my_cache;
        proxy_cache_valid 200 302 10m;
        proxy_cache_use_stale error timeout updating http_500 http_502 http_503 http_504;
        proxy_pass http://backend_api_server:3000/;
        proxy_set_header Host $host;
        proxy_set_header X-Real-IP $remote_addr;
        proxy_set_header X-Forwarded-For $proxy_add_x_forwarded_for;
        proxy_set_header X-Forwarded-Proto $scheme;
    }

    location / {
        root /var/www/your-vue-app/dist;
        try_files $uri $uri/ /index.html;
    }
}
```

In this example, API responses are cached for 10 minutes, which can reduce response times and improve scalability.

Conclusion

Proper server configuration is imperative for the optimal performance and security of Vue.js applications. Whether you are using a basic static file server, setting up a reverse proxy, securing your app with SSL, or implementing caching strategies, each configuration plays a crucial role in the deployment process. Being adept at configuring servers ensures that your Vue applications are not only performant but also robust and secure.

11.3. Deploying to Cloud Providers

When it comes to deploying your Vue.js applications, cloud providers offer a robust, scalable, and reliable infrastructure that can cater to your needs. Common cloud providers include Amazon Web Services (AWS), Google Cloud Platform (GCP), and Microsoft Azure. Each of these platforms offers specific services that can be leveraged for deploying and managing Vue applications. In this subchapter, we will walk you through deploying a Vue application to some of the most popular cloud providers.

Deploying to Amazon Web Services (AWS)

S3 and CloudFront

AWS S3 (Simple Storage Service) can be used to host your Vue application files, while CloudFront can be used as a CDN to serve your application globally.

Step 1: Build Your Vue Application

First, make sure you have built your Vue application:

```
npm run build
```

This will generate the required static files in the `dist` directory.

Step 2: Setup S3 Bucket

1. Log in to the AWS Management Console and go to the S3 service.
2. Create a new bucket and name it, for example, `my-vue-app`.
3. Enable static website hosting. Specify the `index.html` as the index document.

Step 3: Upload Files to S3

Upload the contents of the `dist` directory to your S3 bucket. You can use the AWS CLI for this:

```
aws s3 sync dist/ s3://my-vue-app/
```

Step 4: Configure CloudFront

1. Go to the CloudFront service in the AWS Management Console.
2. Create a new CloudFront distribution and specify the S3 bucket you created earlier as the origin.
3. Take note of the CloudFront distribution URL as this will be the URL you will use to access your application.

Deploying to Google Cloud Platform (GCP)

Google Cloud Storage and Firebase Hosting

Google Cloud Storage can be used to host your Vue application statically. For a more integrated solution, Firebase Hosting is also a great option. Here, we will demonstrate using Firebase Hosting.

Step 1: Build Your Vue Application

```
npm run build
```

Step 2: Install Firebase CLI

You need to install the Firebase CLI for deploying:

```
npm install -g firebase-tools
```

Step 3: Initialize Firebase Project

Log in to Firebase and initialize your project:

```
firebase login
firebase init
```

Select "Hosting" and choose the project you want to deploy. When asked for the "public" directory, specify `dist`.

Step 4: Deploy to Firebase Hosting

```
firebase deploy
```

Take note of the hosting URL provided by Firebase CLI.

Deploying to Microsoft Azure

Azure Storage and Azure App Service

Azure Storage can be used to serve static files, while Azure App Service offers a more comprehensive solution for dynamic applications.

Step 1: Build Your Vue Application

```
npm run build
```

Step 2: Create a Storage Account

1. Log in to the Azure Portal.
2. Create a new resource and select "Storage Account."
3. Create a container in the storage account, for example, vue-app.

Step 3: Upload Files to Azure Blob Storage

You can use Azure CLI to upload your files:

```
az storage blob upload-batch -s ./dist -d vue-app --account-name <your_storage_account_name>
```

Step 4: Setup Static Website Hosting

1. Navigate to Static website in your storage account.
2. Enable Static website hosting and set `index.html` as the index document.
3. Note the primary endpoint URL, which will be used to access your application.

Conclusion

Deploying Vue.js applications to cloud providers involves a series of steps that include preparing your production build, configuring cloud services, and ensuring proper hosting settings. Each cloud provider offers unique services and tools, making it essential to understand their specific configurations. By leveraging cloud solutions, your Vue applications will benefit from enhanced scalability, availability, and performance.

11.4. Continuous Deployment with CI/CD

Continuous Deployment (CD) is a development practice where code changes are automatically deployed to production after they pass through various stages of testing and quality assurance. Incorporating Continuous Integration (CI) with CD ensures that every code commit is verified with automated tests before being deployed. This subchapter explores how to set up Continuous Deployment with CI/CD for Vue applications, making your deployment process more efficient and reliable.

Benefits of CI/CD

- **Automation:** Reduces manual intervention, speeding up the deployment process.
- **Consistency:** Ensures that the deployment process is uniform, minimizing errors.
- **Feedback:** Provides immediate feedback on build and test statuses.
- **Scalability:** Makes it easier to manage multiple environments and scaling issues.

Tools for CI/CD

Several tools are available for setting up CI/CD pipelines for Vue applications, including:

- **Jenkins**
- **GitHub Actions**
- **GitLab CI**
- **CircleCI**

- Travis CI

In this subchapter, we'll focus on GitHub Actions due to its tight integration with GitHub repositories and ease of use.

Setting Up GitHub Actions

To set up GitHub Actions for a Vue application, follow these steps:

1. **Create a .github Directory:** In the root of your repository, create a `.github` directory with a `workflows` subdirectory.

    ```
    mkdir -p .github/workflows
    ```

2. **Create a Workflow File:** Create a new YAML file for your workflow, e.g., `ci-cd.yml`.

    ```
    touch .github/workflows/ci-cd.yml
    ```

3. **Define Your Workflow:** Open the `ci-cd.yml` file and define your CI/CD pipeline. Here's a basic example:

    ```yaml
    name: CI/CD Pipeline

    on:
      push:
        branches:
          - main
      pull_request:
        branches:
          - main

    jobs:
      build:
        runs-on: ubuntu-latest

        steps:
          - name: Checkout code
            uses: actions/checkout@v2

          - name: Set up Node.js
            uses: actions/setup-node@v2
            with:
    ```

```yaml
        node-version: '14'

      - name: Install dependencies
        run: npm install

      - name: Run tests
        run: npm test

      - name: Build Vue app
        run: npm run build

      - name: Deploy to Production
        if: github.ref == 'refs/heads/main'
        run: |
          echo "Deploying to production server"
          # Add your deployment scripts here
```

Deployment to Production

The deployment step can vary depending on your hosting provider. Here are some common scenarios:

Deploy to Firebase Hosting

1. **Set Up Firebase CLI:** Ensure you have Firebase CLI installed and authenticated.

   ```
   npm install -g firebase-tools
   firebase login
   ```

2. **Modify Workflow for Firebase Hosting:** Update the `ci-cd.yml` file to include deployment to Firebase.

   ```yaml
   - name: Deploy to Firebase Hosting
     run: |
       npm install -g firebase-tools
       firebase deploy --token $FIREBASE_TOKEN
   ```

   Make sure to set the `FIREBASE_TOKEN` in your GitHub repository's secrets.

Deploy to AWS S3 and CloudFront

1. **Set Up AWS CLI:** Ensure you have AWS CLI installed and configured.

   ```
   pip install awscli
   aws configure
   ```

2. **Modify Workflow for AWS S3:** Update the `ci-cd.yml` file to include deployment to AWS S3.

   ```
   - name: Deploy to S3
     run: |
       aws s3 sync dist/ s3://your-bucket-name --delete
   ```

   Make sure to set AWS credentials in your GitHub repository's secrets.

Conclusion

Setting up a CI/CD pipeline for your Vue application streamlines the deployment process and allows you to focus on development rather than manual deployment chores. Using GitHub Actions, you can easily automate your workflow from building to testing and finally deploying your Vue application to production.

12. Glossary

Glossary

Vue.js

Vue.js is a progressive JavaScript framework used for building user interfaces and single-page applications. It is designed to be incrementally adoptable, focusing on the view layer and can be easily integrated into big projects for front-end development.

Vue CLI

Vue Command Line Interface (CLI) is a standard tooling for Vue.js development. It provides extensive functionality for building, developing, and managing Vue.js projects, including project scaffolding, configuration, and instant prototyping.

Vue Components

Vue Components are reusable Vue instances with a name. Components allow the modularization of the code, making the applications easier to maintain and scale. Each component encapsulates its structure, style, and behavior.

Vuex

Vuex is a state management library for Vue.js applications. It serves as a central store for all the components in an application, facilitating a robust way of managing shared state or data flow across the application.

Vue Router

Vue Router is the official router for Vue.js, used to create single-page applications with multiple views. It maps routes to components, allowing developers to build navigation across the application.

Directives

Directives are special tokens in the markup that tell the library to do something to a DOM element. Vue.js has built-in directives like v-bind, v-model, and v-for, which extend HTML's functionality in ways more expressive and readable.

Filters

Filters in Vue.js are used to format or transform data displayed to the user. They are primarily used to apply common text formatting like capitalization, date formatting, etc., within templates.

Mixins

Mixins in Vue.js allow you to define a piece of reusable functionality that can be included within components. They enable reusing code across multiple components, combining lifecycle hooks, methods, and others.

Forms

Handling forms in Vue involves managing user input, validation, and submission. Vue provides directives such as v-model for two-way data binding, making it straightforward to keep form data in sync with the component's state.

User Input

User input handling in Vue.js involves capturing and responding to the user's actions. Vue provides event handlers like v-on for binding users' events such as clicks, input changes, and form submissions to methods.

Laravel

Laravel is a comprehensive PHP framework used for building robust backend applications. Integrating Vue with Laravel involves combining Vue's reactive components with Laravel's backend functionalities to create full-stack web applications.

Backend Frameworks

Backend frameworks like Laravel, Express, Django, and Rails are server-side frameworks that facilitate the development of web servers and APIs. Integrating these with Vue.js allows for an effective separation of concerns between front-end and back-end development.

Testing

Testing in Vue.js refers to ensuring the correctness of the application through unit tests, integration tests, and end-to-end tests. This is typically performed using tools like Jest, Mocha, and Cypress.

Debugging

Debugging in Vue involves identifying and fixing errors in the application. Tools like Vue Devtools provide an enhanced debugging experience by offering features for inspecting and editing component states, events, and much more.

Performance Optimization

Performance optimization in Vue.js involves practices aimed at improving the rendering and responsiveness of Vue applications. Techniques include lazy loading, code-splitting, using virtual scroll, and optimizing reactivity to manage resource-heavy tasks efficiently.

Deployment

Deploying Vue applications involves preparing the application for production and making it available to the end users. It includes building the production-ready code, configuring the server, and using CI/CD pipelines and cloud platforms like AWS, Heroku, or Netlify.

Glossary

A glossary is a section in a book that provides definitions or explanations of terms frequently used in the text. The glossary for "Practical Vue.js for Modern Web Development" includes detailed definitions relevant to Vue.js and associated broader contexts.

www.ingramcontent.com/pod-product-compliance
Lightning Source LLC
Chambersburg PA
CBHW052310220526
45472CB00001B/58